REJECT

In

The

CHURCH

DR. RICHELLE MCMILLAN

Rejection in the Church Copyright © 2024 by Dr. Richelle McMillan Enterprise, LLC
Published by: Richelle McMillan Enterprise, LLC
Printed in the United States of America

ISBN: 9798324849108

All rights reserved. This book or any portion thereof may not be reproduced or used in any manner whatsoever without the express written permission of the publisher except for the use of brief quotations in a book review. For additional information, email Dr. Richelle McMillan.
Richelle.mcmilan@yahoo.com

Disclaimer: It's important to note that this rejection manual is not intended to provide medical advice. While it offers guidance, coping strategies, and insights into navigating rejection, it's essential to consult with a qualified healthcare professional or therapist for personalized support and advice. The manual serves as a resource to empower individuals to understand and cope with rejection more effectively, but it is not a substitute for professional medical or psychological treatment. If you're struggling with rejection and its impact on your mental health, please seek support from a licensed therapist or counselor who can offer personalized guidance and support.

First Printing, 2024
Available from Amazon.com and other retail outlets
Cover Design & Images: Maria Corina

Scripture quotations are taken from the KING JAMES VERSION (KJV): KING JAMES VERSION, public domain. Scripture quotations marked (NIV) are taken from the Holy Bible, New International Version., NIV. Copyright © 1973, 1978, 1984, 2011 by Biblica, Inc. Used by permission of Zondervan. All rights reserved worldwide. www.zondervan.com The NIV and New International Version are trademarks registered in the United States Patent and Trademark Office by Biblica, Inc.

Dedication

There are so many people in my life who had a great impact on my writing this book. The task of trying to acknowledge all the phenomenal people who have in some fashion morph this book isn't easy but, I will give it a try! First, the Lord is the author and finisher of my faith and this project. Let me express a heartfelt appreciation to my beautiful, blessed beauties, Joy and Ja'chelle for trusting me with being there mother and willingness to grow with me as an aspiring author. Secondly, to the key people who pray, mentored, coach, cried, and generously shared with me in many life experiences: Apostle Eugene & Pastor Karen Durant, EP Lila Adams, Apostle Audrea Abraham, Dr. Renee Thompson, SDSMovement, and my beautiful family across the world. Lastly, this is a dream come true and I want to extend my deepest gratitude to all the women and men for inspiring me make peace with painful memories and live a fulling life.

Contents

Dedication 3
Introduction 10
What is Rejection? 11
What is Rejection in the Church? 12
What is Church Rejection? 12
The Evolution of Church Rejection 14
Church Rejection Scenario 15
Rejection Root Causes 16
History of Church Rejection! 17
Psychology of Rejection 18
Church Rejection Model (CRM) 19
Comprehensive Framework of the Church Rejection Model (CRM) 20
Summary 21
Theoretical Foundations of the Church Rejection Model (CRM) 22
Conclusion 23
CRM Theological Principles 24
Conclusion 25
CRM Key Components 26
Conclusion 27
Key Factors Contributing to 28
Rejection in the Church 28
Conclusion 29
Church Rejection Key Factors 30
Rejection Scenario 32
CRM Rejection Reflection 33
Church Rejection Model Dynamics 34
Church Dynamics of Rejection 36
Interpersonal and Structural 36
What are Interpersonal and Structural Church Dynamics of Church Rejection? 37
Summary 40
Church Rejection Model Hidden Biases and Power Imbalances 41

CRM Rejection Reflection	43
CRM Psychological, Emotional, and Spiritual Consequences	44
Church Rejection	45
Psychological Impact	45
Church Rejection Psychological Impact Definitions	46
Church Rejection Psychological Scenarios	47
Scenario I: Devoted Church Member	47
Scenario II: Church Member	48
Scenario III: Church Member	49
Scenario III: Pastor Wife	50
Scenario IV: Choir Member	51
Summary	51
Church Rejection	52
Emotional Impact	52
Church Rejection	53
Emotional Impact	53
Church Rejection Emotional Impact Definitions	54
Church Rejection	55
Emotional Scenarios	55
Scenario I: Pastor	55
Scenario II: Deacon	56
Scenario II: Married Couple	57
Scenario III: Usher	58
Summary	59
Church Rejection	60
Spiritual Impact	60
Church Rejection Spiritual Impact Definition	60
Church Rejection	61
Spiritual Impact	61
Church Rejection Spiritual Impact Definitions	62
Church Rejection	63
Spiritual Impact	63
Church Rejection	64
Spiritual Impact Scenarios	64
Scenario I: Sunday School Teacher	64
Scenario II: Church Musician	65

Scenario III: Youth Leader	66
SUMMARY	67
Rejection	68
Understanding Rejection Mental Disorders	69
What are Mental Disorders?	69
Rejection Related Disorders	70
Rejection Related Disorders	72
Types and Characteristics	72
Rejection Related Disorders Scenario	73
Scenario I: Armourbearer	73
Scenario II: Pastor's Children	74
Scenario III: Bishop	75
Scenario IV: Prophetess	76
Scenario V: Executive Pastor	77
Rejection Mindset	78
Church Rejection Mindset	79
Church Rejection Mindset Scenario	80
Church Rejection Mindset Scenario	81
Summary	82
Church Rejection Triggers	83
Church Rejection Types of Triggers	84
Church Rejection Triggers & Factors	85
Common Church Rejection Triggers	86
Speech Patterns:	87
Body Language:	87
Church Rejection Triggers Scenario	88
Scenario I: Parishioner	88
Church Rejection In Women and Men	89
Summary	90
Church Rejections Impacts	91
Brain Development	91
Church Rejection Catastrophizing	93
Church	94
Rejection	94
Strategies	94
Church Rejection Techniques	95

Church Rejection Common Failures	95
Church Rejection Common Errors	97
Church Rejection Summary	98
Dealing with Church Rejection	99
Church Rejection Biblical Perspective	100
Understanding Rejection in Church Leadership	101
Sources of Church Rejection	101
Impact of Rejection on Church Leaders' Well-being and Effectiveness	101
Effects of Rejection on Church Leaders	102
Biblical Perspective on Rejection for Church Leaders	104
Church Rejection Strategies	106
Church Rejection Coping Strategies	107
Professionally:	107
In Relationships:	107
With Family:	108
Internally:	108
Coping Strategies for Church Leaders Facing Rejection	109
Church Rejection Coping Strategies Checklist	111
Church Rejection Coping Checklist	112
Church Rejection Coping Strategies for Leaders	113
Church leadership	114
Rejection Scenario	114
Scenario I: Audrea's Journey Through Rejection	114
Scenario II: Audrea's Journey Through Rejection and Coping Strategies	115
Summary	116
Dealing with Church Rejection	117
Guidelines for Effective Deliverances from Church Rejection	118
Summary	119
Defeating Church Rejection Scriptures	120
Summary	121
Rejection Self-Help Exercises	122
Church Rejection Self-Help Exercises	123
Church Rejection Exercises Implementation	124
SUMMARY	125
Church Rejection Exercises	126

Rejection Prevention and Control	127
SUMMARY	128
Church Rejection Management Plan	129
PREVENTIVE	130
SOLUTIONS	130
Leaving a Church Effectively after Rejection	132
Departing a Church Following Rejection:	132
Summary	133
Leaving a Church Gracefully Following Experience of Rejection	134
Summary	134
Social Media Etiquette When Departing from a Church	135
Church Rejection Action Plans	136
Handling Church Rejection Using an Action Plan	136
Leadership Skills	137
Responding to Church Rejection	137
Building Resilience in Church Leadership	138
Summary	139
Navigating Church Rejection:	140
Do's and Don't	140
Summary	141
Church Rejection Signs	142
Church Rejection	143
Critical Conversations	143
Navigating Critical Conversations About Church Rejection	143
Summary	144
Rejection Tip & Techniques	146
Rejection in the Workplace	147
Rejection FREE Work Culture	148
Rejection Free Family Dynamics Solutions	149
SUMMARY	150
Rejection Work-Life Balance Solutions	151
SUMMARY	152
Rejection Routine Care Solutions	153
SUMMARY	153
Rejection Free Environment	154
Dealing with Rejection	155

Do and Don't	155
Rejection Critical Conversation Solutions	156
Breaking Rejection Cycle	157
Rejection Breathing Techniques	159
Rejection Breathing Exercises Benefits	160
Rejection Technique	161
SUMMARY	162
Reject Rejection	163
Stop Rejection	163
Rejection Normalization Cards	163
SUMMARY	164
Church Rejection Rules	165
Church Rejection Diary Worksheet	166
Building Tolerance for Church Rejection	167
Church Rejection Summary	167
Rejection	168
Questionnaire	168
The Rejection Triggers Questionnaire	169
Rejection Triggers Questionnaire	170
SUMMARY	171
Resources	172
About the Author	173

Introduction

As I became an adult, I learned the ability to handle a normal amount of stress when it comes to work but not so much when it came to matters of the heart. The last relationship pushed me beyond my wildest limitations. The problem emerged little and as the years went on the rejection and meltdowns were creating levels of physical, mental and emotional strains day after day. One day, I looked in the mirror combing my natural hair and it was coming out in patches. It wasn't until then that I realized that the weight of my everyday life was exceeding my limits, and trouble was on the horizon.

Everyone has felt stressed out or experienced rejection. Rejection is a normal part of everyday life, is what I thought. It wasn't until I went to see a doctor for experiencing chest pains and hair loss. I was constantly sick every couple of weeks, and no one could determine what was wrong. Then I realized that rejection was more than a fragment of my imagination and was becoming a stronghold in my life. The fear of rejection had gained a foothold that walked in my life through people that had access to my vulnerability. It wasn't until years later that the Lord used this nurse to tell me, that I was running from myself and needed to deal with the real issues in your current relationship. She said it was time to be Real with myself and stop running from your issues. What a harsh but sincere word! Was, I am running from myself so much that it was impacting my health. I had to take a closer look at myself and release the fear of rejection that was happening in my life.

My story is just a sample of billions who encounter similar encounters ignoring the signs of rejections. This book is designed to describe the characteristics of rejection, and to show you how to faith in God will bring you the victory. It's time to flush it out of your life and begin to life a Rejection free live every day.

Confidence is the sole outcome of this book. No matter your age, no matter your walk of life or social status. This book is designed to help you with overcoming rejection and dealing with the underlying problems of how to get outside of your comfort zone. As you begin to engage in stepping out your comfort zone you will begin addressing issues from many different angles to get different types of results. Get equipped with these twelve strategies that will provide the antidote to fueling your happiness.

What is Rejection?

Rejection is the act of refusing to accept, consider, or approve of something or someone. It involves dismissing or declining a proposal, request, idea, or individual, often based on perceived inadequacies, differences, or preferences. Rejection can occur in various contexts, including interpersonal relationships, professional settings, social interactions, and personal endeavors. It can elicit feelings of disappointment, hurt, or sadness in those who experience it, and it may have significant emotional, psychological, and social implications. **Rejection** can transcend across cultures, traditions, and religions. Many social, political, and economic realities influence the diverse path of rejection for people. To understand how Rejection fits in your lives, you must have a clear picture of the nature of the term and the importance of transferring the knowledge to your lives. There are many meanings centered around Rejection. The Webster definition for the term *rejection* refers to the "actual act of rejecting something or to the feeling one has after being rejected" by someone. Rejection changes your mood, thoughts, beliefs and attitude that can lead to emotional instability. The basic notion is that rejection heightens the way you think and changes your response to various situations. In other words, you measure your confidence and identity by how much you do for others and how they treat you. Rejection can lead to universal acceptances that is rooted in people pleasing behaviors. The awareness of understanding the various views of rejection will help you understand the options you have in determining the strategies needed in various situations. The basic idea of rejection can be expressed in various ways:

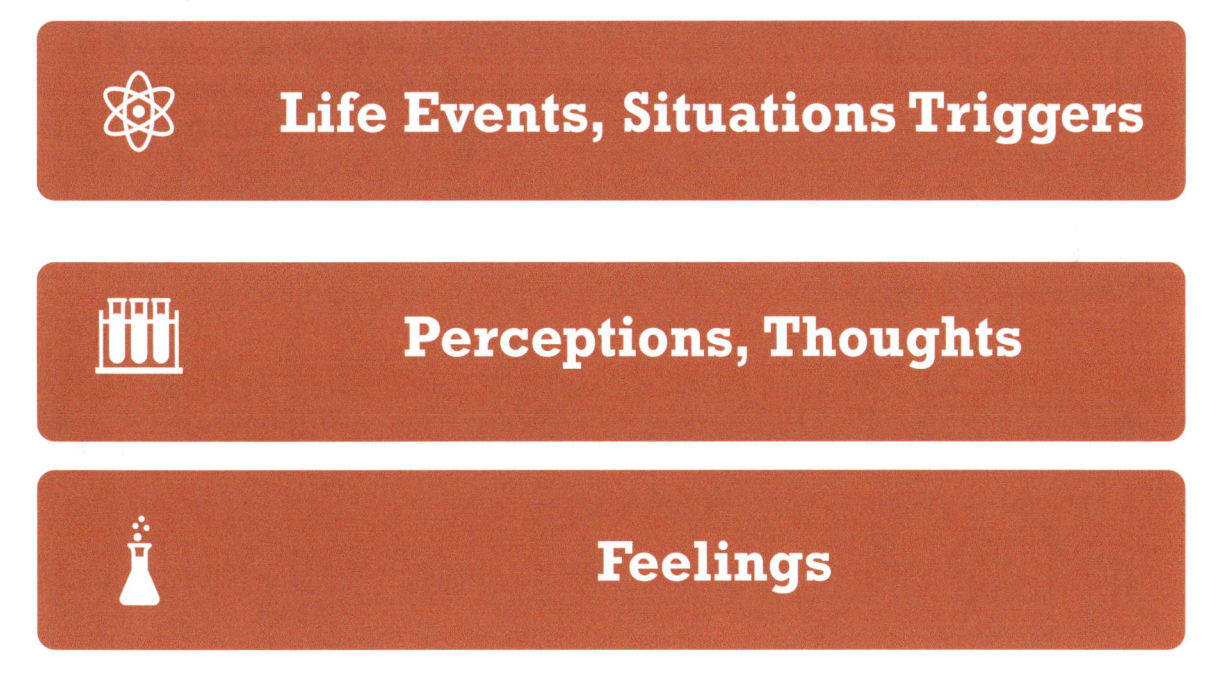

- **Life Events, Situations Triggers**
- **Perceptions, Thoughts**
- **Feelings**

As you can see, Rejection can be driven by thoughts, behaviors, and feelings. The way you think, and process information has a great impact on you coming to terms with Rejection. Clearly, Rejection is no beign problem. Simply, review the example below to develop your awareness of the problem and think about techniques of recovery.

What is Rejection in the Church?

Rejection in the church refers to the experience of being excluded, dismissed, or marginalized within the religious community. It encompasses various forms of social, emotional, or spiritual alienation, stemming from differences in beliefs, practices, identities, or interpersonal dynamics. Rejection in the church can manifest in exclusion from social activities, judgmental attitudes, doctrinal disputes, or discrimination based on factors such as race, gender, or sexual orientation. It undermines the core values of love, acceptance, and inclusivity taught by many faith traditions and can have profound effects on individuals' sense of belonging, faith, and emotional well-being within the church community. Addressing rejection in the church involves fostering empathy, understanding, and reconciliation, and creating an environment where all members feel valued, respected, and welcomed as integral parts of the body of Christ.

What is Church Rejection?

Church rejection refers to the experience of being dismissed, excluded, or marginalized within the context of a religious community. It can manifest in various forms, including:

1. **Social exclusion**: Feeling left out or isolated from church activities, groups, or events.
2. **Spiritual rejection**: Being made to feel unwelcome or judged based on one's beliefs, practices, or spiritual experiences.
3. **Emotional rejection:** Experiencing criticism, invalidation, or lack of empathy from church members or leaders.
4. **Exclusion from leadership or service opportunities:** Being denied opportunities to contribute or participate in church leadership, ministry, or service activities.

Church rejection can have profound effects on individuals' sense of belonging, faith, and emotional well-being. It may lead to feelings of loneliness, doubt, anger, or disillusionment with the church community and its teachings. Addressing church rejection involves creating a culture of inclusivity, empathy, and acceptance within the church, where all members feel valued and respected as integral parts of the body of Christ.

Within the sacred walls of religious communities, where the bonds of fellowship and faith are meant to be unbreakable, the specter of rejection can cast a shadow over the hearts of believers. In the realm of the church, rejection manifests in various forms, each leaving its own indelible mark on the souls of those who experience it.

1. **Social Exclusion:** Social exclusion within the church strikes at the very core of one's sense of belonging and community. It is the feeling of being on the outside looking in, as others gather in fellowship and communion. Whether it's being left out of church activities, groups, or events, social exclusion can evoke profound feelings of loneliness, isolation, and alienation.
2. **Spiritual Rejection:** In the sacred space of the church, one would hope to find solace and acceptance for their spiritual journey. However, spiritual rejection can shatter this illusion, leaving individuals feeling unwelcome or judged based on their beliefs, practices, or spiritual experiences. Whether it's being labeled as too liberal or too conservative, spiritual rejection undermines the very essence of religious faith and community.
3. **Emotional Rejection:** Emotional rejection within the church cuts deep, striking at the heart of one's emotional well-being and self-worth. It is the experience of being met with criticism, invalidation, or a lack of empathy from fellow church members or leaders. Whether it's feeling misunderstood, dismissed, or belittled, emotional rejection can erode trust, confidence, and resilience.
4. **Exclusion from Leadership or Service Opportunities:** Within the church, opportunities for leadership and service are meant to be pathways to spiritual growth and fulfillment. However, exclusion from these opportunities can hinder one's sense of purpose and contribution within the faith community. Whether it's being denied the chance to lead, minister, or serve based on arbitrary criteria or biases, exclusion from leadership or service opportunities can breed resentment, disillusionment, and disengagement.

The Evolution of Church Rejection

Within the intricate tapestry of human interactions, rejection reveals itself in myriad forms, each leaving its own unique imprint on the hearts and minds of those who experience it. In the sacred spaces of religious communities, where the promise of love, acceptance, and belonging is meant to be most profound, the sting of rejection can be particularly poignant. To truly understand the depth and complexity of rejection within the church, we must explore its manifestations in various scenarios, each shedding light on the ways in which rejection can fracture the bonds of fellowship and faith.

Certainly, here are examples of each way rejection can manifest within the church context:

1. **Social Exclusion:** Example: Sarah, a newcomer to the church, eagerly attends Sunday services and Bible studies, hoping to connect with fellow believers. However, she notices that she is consistently left out of social gatherings and fellowship opportunities. Despite her efforts to engage with others, she feels increasingly isolated and excluded from the church community, leading her to question whether she truly belongs.
2. **Spiritual Rejection:** Example: James, a long-time member of the church, begins to express doubts about certain theological beliefs held by the congregation. Rather than engaging in thoughtful dialogue or seeking understanding, James is met with skepticism and judgment from fellow church members. He feels ostracized and misunderstood, as if his questions and struggles are not welcome within the community of faith.
3. **Emotional Rejection:** Example: Emily, a dedicated volunteer in the church, offers her time and talents to serve in various ministries. However, she consistently receives harsh criticism and micromanagement from church leaders, who fail to acknowledge her contributions or show empathy for her efforts. Feeling unappreciated and undervalued, Emily becomes disheartened and begins to withdraw from active involvement in the church.
4. **Exclusion from Leadership or Service Opportunities:** Example: David, a passionate young member of the church, expresses interest in leading a new outreach initiative aimed at serving the local community. However, when he presents his proposal to church leadership, he is dismissed without consideration, citing his lack of experience or perceived inadequacies. Despite his enthusiasm and willingness to serve, David is denied the opportunity to contribute in a meaningful way, leaving him feeling disillusioned and sidelined within the church.

Church Rejection Scenario

1. **Social Exclusion:** In this scenario, we witness the subtle yet profound ways in which social exclusion can erode the sense of belonging and community within the church. Through the lens of Sarah's experience, we gain insight into the loneliness and isolation that accompany being on the outside looking in, as others gather in fellowship and communion. Sarah's story serves as a poignant reminder of the importance of inclusivity and hospitality within the church, and the devastating impact of exclusion on the spiritual well-being of individuals.
2. **Spiritual Rejection:** Through James's journey, we explore the complexities of spiritual rejection within the church context. James's doubts and questions are met not with openness and understanding, but with skepticism and judgment, leaving him feeling alienated and misunderstood. His experience highlights the delicate balance between faith and doubt, and the need for grace and humility in engaging with those who grapple with theological uncertainties.
3. **Emotional Rejection:** Emily's story unveils the emotional toll of rejection within the church, as she grapples with criticism and invalidation from church leaders. Her dedication and service are met not with appreciation and support, but with harsh judgment and indifference, leading her to question her worth and purpose within the community of faith. Through Emily's experience, we confront the damaging effects of emotional rejection on individuals' self-esteem and well-being, and the urgent need for empathy and compassion in our interactions with one another.
4. **Exclusion from Leadership or Service Opportunities:** David's journey exposes the barriers to inclusion and participation within the church, as he faces rejection in his pursuit of leadership and service opportunities. Despite his passion and enthusiasm, David encounters resistance and dismissal from church leadership, who fail to recognize his potential and value as a member of the community. His experience underscores the importance of dismantling systemic barriers to participation and empowerment within the church, and the transformative power of embracing diversity and inclusion in all aspects of church life.

Through these examples, we are invited to confront the reality of rejection within the church and to reflect on our own roles in fostering a culture of acceptance, belonging, and grace. May they serve as catalysts for dialogue, empathy, and reconciliation within our communities of faith, as we strive to embody the boundless love and compassion of our Creator. In the pages that follow, we will delve deeper into each of these forms of rejection within the church, exploring their root causes, their impact on individuals and communities, and the pathways to healing, reconciliation, and renewal. Through empathy, understanding, and a commitment to love and inclusion, we can begin to address the pervasive issue of rejection within the church and build communities that reflect the boundless grace and acceptance of the divine.

Rejection Root Causes

Rejection, with its sharp sting and lingering ache, is a universal human experience that transcends boundaries of age, culture, and circumstance. It is a multifaceted phenomenon that can manifest in a myriad of forms, each leaving its own distinct imprint on the human psyche. In the realm of relationships, work, and society at large, rejection can cast a shadow over our sense of self-worth, belonging, and identity.

Within the intricate tapestry of human interactions, rejection takes on many shapes and colors, each revealing something profound about the human condition. It can be overt, as in the case of a harsh word or outright dismissal, or it can be subtle, lurking in the silent gaps between words and actions. It can be personal, targeting our deepest insecurities and vulnerabilities, or it can be systemic, embedded within the structures and institutions that govern our lives.

In the sacred spaces of religious communities, where the promise of love, acceptance, and belonging looms large, rejection can be particularly poignant. Whether it takes the form of exclusion from social activities, judgmental attitudes, or doctrinal disputes, rejection within the context of the church can shake the very foundations of one's faith and sense of belonging.

Yet, despite its ubiquity and potency, rejection is not an insurmountable obstacle. It is a challenge to be confronted, a wound to be tended with care and compassion. By understanding the various forms in which rejection can manifest, we can begin to unravel its complexities and chart a course towards healing, reconciliation, and renewal.

In the pages that follow, we will explore the myriad ways in which rejection can manifest in our lives and communities. We will delve into the psychological, emotional, and spiritual dimensions of rejection, examining its impact on individuals and societies alike. And, perhaps most importantly, we will seek to uncover the pathways to resilience, empathy, and understanding that can help us navigate the tumultuous waters of rejection with grace and courage.

History of Church Rejection!

The history of church rejection is deeply intertwined with the evolution of religious beliefs, practices, and institutions throughout the centuries. While organized religion has often served as a source of solace, community, and spiritual guidance for many, it has also been a site of conflict, division, and exclusion.

One of the earliest examples of church rejection can be found in the New Testament of the Bible, where Jesus Christ himself faced rejection from religious authorities and societal elites of his time. Despite his teachings of love, compassion, and inclusion, Jesus was often met with skepticism, hostility, and ultimately, betrayal and crucifixion.

Throughout the history of Christianity, the church has been both a source of refuge for the marginalized and a perpetrator of exclusion and discrimination. During the early centuries of the church, doctrinal disputes and theological controversies led to the excommunication and persecution of those deemed heretical or non-conforming to established orthodoxy.

The medieval period saw the rise of the Catholic Church as a dominant religious and political institution in Europe. While the church provided stability and unity in a time of political upheaval, it also wielded immense power and authority, often at the expense of individual freedoms and religious diversity. Those who challenged the church's teachings or authority, such as the Protestant reformers, were met with harsh repression and persecution.

The Protestant Reformation of the 16th century brought about significant theological and ecclesiastical changes within Christianity, leading to the emergence of various Protestant denominations. However, the reformers themselves were not immune to perpetuating rejection, as they often persecuted dissenting voices within their own ranks and against Catholics.

Colonialism and the spread of Christianity to other parts of the world also brought with it a legacy of church rejection. Indigenous peoples, cultures, and religions were often marginalized, oppressed, and forcibly converted in the name of Christianization, leading to profound social, cultural, and spiritual upheaval.

In more recent history, the church has grappled with issues of exclusion and discrimination related to race, gender, sexuality, and other identity markers. The civil rights movement, women's liberation movement, and LGBTQ+ rights movement have all challenged the church to confront its complicity in perpetuating systems of inequality and injustice.

Despite its history of rejection, the church has also been a site of resilience, transformation, and reconciliation. Many individuals and communities within the church have worked tirelessly to challenge oppressive systems, promote social justice, and create spaces of welcome and inclusion for all.

Today, the church continues to wrestle with issues of rejection, inclusion, and diversity within its ranks. As it navigates the complexities of a rapidly changing world, the church must strive to embody the principles of love, compassion, and justice that lie at the heart of the Christian faith, working towards a more inclusive and equitable community for all.

Psychology of Rejection

The psychology of rejection delves into the multifaceted ways in which humans perceive, experience, and respond to rejection. It encompasses a range of emotional, cognitive, and behavioral processes that shape individuals' reactions to rejection, as well as its impact on their mental and emotional well-being.

1. **Emotional Responses:** Rejection often elicits a strong emotional response, including feelings of sadness, anger, shame, and fear. These emotions can vary depending on factors such as the context of the rejection, the individual's attachment style, and their past experiences with rejection. For example, individuals with a history of repeated rejection may develop a heightened sensitivity to rejection and experience more intense emotional reactions.
2. **Cognitive Appraisals:** How individuals interpret and make sense of rejection plays a crucial role in shaping their psychological response. Negative cognitive appraisals, such as interpreting rejection as a reflection of one's inadequacy or unworthiness, can contribute to feelings of low self-esteem and self-blame. On the other hand, more adaptive appraisals, such as viewing rejection as a temporary setback or as a reflection of the other person's preferences or circumstances, can help individuals maintain a sense of resilience and self-worth.
3. **Self-Esteem and Identity:** Rejection can have significant implications for individuals' self-esteem and sense of identity. A perceived lack of acceptance or approval from others can undermine one's self-esteem and lead to feelings of insecurity or self-doubt. Repeated experiences of rejection can also shape individuals' self-concept and identity, influencing how they perceive themselves and their place in the world.
4. **Social and Interpersonal Dynamics:** Rejection can impact individuals' social relationships and interpersonal dynamics in various ways. It may lead to withdrawal or avoidance of social interactions as a way to protect oneself from further rejection. Alternatively, it can trigger behaviors aimed at seeking reassurance or validation from others, sometimes leading to overdependence or clinginess in relationships. Rejection can also influence how individuals perceive and trust others, affecting their ability to form new connections or maintain existing ones.
5. **Coping Mechanisms:** Individuals employ various coping mechanisms to manage the distress associated with rejection. Some may engage in problem-focused coping strategies, such as seeking social support, engaging in activities that boost self-esteem, or actively addressing the source of rejection. Others may use emotion-focused coping strategies, such as distraction, avoidance, or seeking comfort from internal sources (e.g., self-soothing techniques). The effectiveness of these coping mechanisms can vary depending on individual differences and the specific context of the rejection.

Overall, the psychology of rejection highlights the complex interplay of emotions, cognitions, and behaviors that shape individuals' experiences and responses to rejection. By understanding these processes, psychologists can develop interventions and strategies to help individuals cope with rejection more effectively and build resilience in the face of adversity.

Church Rejection Model (CRM)

In the sacred spaces of religious communities, where the echoes of prayer and song mingle with the shared aspirations of faith, one might expect to find solace, acceptance, and unity. And yet, within the hallowed halls of the church, a shadow often lurks—a shadow cast by the specter of rejection.

The Church Rejection Model represents an earnest endeavor to confront this uncomfortable reality head-on, to dissect the intricate web of factors, dynamics, and consequences that underlie rejection within religious communities, and to chart a course towards healing, reconciliation, and renewal.

At its core, the Church Rejection Model seeks to provide a comprehensive framework for understanding the complex interplay of forces that give rise to rejection within the church. It is a roadmap that guides us through the labyrinth of doctrinal disputes, social hierarchies, cultural biases, and interpersonal conflicts that shape the landscape of rejection within religious communities.

But the Church Rejection Model is more than just a theoretical construct—it is a call to action, a clarion call for introspection, empathy, and transformation within the church. It challenges us to confront the uncomfortable truths that lie at the heart of rejection, to acknowledge the pain and suffering it inflicts, and to muster the courage and compassion necessary to address it.

In the pages that follow, we will embark on a journey of discovery—a journey that takes us deep into the heart of rejection within the church, but also towards the promise of healing, reconciliation, and redemption. We will explore the myriad ways in which rejection manifests within religious communities, the profound impact it has on individuals and communities alike, and the strategies and interventions that hold the potential to bring about positive change.

But more than that, the Church Rejection Model is a testament to the enduring hope that lies at the heart of the Christian faith—the hope that, even in the face of rejection, we are never alone, for we serve a God who is intimately acquainted with our pain and who longs to bring healing and wholeness to all who are hurting.

May this model serve as a guiding light for all who seek to confront rejection within the church, leading us towards a future where love, acceptance, and grace reign supreme, and where all are welcomed, valued, and embraced as beloved children of God.

Comprehensive Framework of the Church Rejection Model (CRM)

The Church Rejection Model (CRM) represents a comprehensive framework for understanding the multifaceted nature of rejection within religious communities. Grounded in principles of empathy, inclusivity, and reconciliation, CRM seeks to unravel the intricate web of factors, dynamics, and consequences that underlie rejection within the church context. In this chapter, we will explore the key components of CRM, providing insight into its theoretical foundations, practical applications, and implications for fostering healing and renewal within religious communities.

1. **Theoretical Foundations of CRM:**
   - CRM draws upon insights from psychology, sociology, theology, and pastoral care to inform its theoretical framework.
   - Psychological theories of attachment, social identity, and cognitive appraisal provide insight into the emotional, cognitive, and interpersonal dimensions of rejection.
   - Sociological perspectives on power dynamics, social exclusion, and group dynamics illuminate the social and structural factors that contribute to rejection within religious communities.
   - Theological principles of love, grace, and reconciliation serve as guiding principles for addressing rejection within the context of faith.
2. **Key Components of CRM:** a. Identification of Rejection Factors:
   - CRM begins by identifying key factors contributing to rejection within the church, including doctrinal differences, social hierarchies, cultural biases, and interpersonal conflicts.
   - By understanding the root causes of rejection, CRM seeks to address systemic issues and promote a culture of inclusivity and belonging within religious communities.

   b. **Formation of Rejection Dynamics:**
   - CRM explores how rejection manifests within church settings through various dynamics such as exclusion from social activities, judgmental attitudes, discrimination, or marginalization.
   - By examining the interpersonal and structural dynamics of rejection, CRM seeks to uncover hidden biases and power imbalances that perpetuate exclusion and division.

   c. **Impact on Individuals and Communities:**
   - CRM examines the psychological, emotional, and spiritual consequences of rejection within the church, including effects on self-esteem, identity formation, mental health, and sense of belonging.
   - By acknowledging the human cost of rejection, CRM underscores the importance of fostering empathy, understanding, and support for those who have been marginalized or excluded.

3. **Practical Applications of CRM:**
   - CRM offers practical strategies and interventions for addressing rejection within religious communities, including education and awareness campaigns, training on inclusivity and empathy, and conflict resolution skills.
   - By implementing evidence-based practices informed by CRM, religious leaders and community members can create environments that promote healing, reconciliation, and renewal for all individuals affected by rejection.
4. **Implications for Healing and Renewal:**
   - CRM holds profound implications for fostering healing and renewal within religious communities, as it provides a framework for confronting the uncomfortable truths of rejection and working towards reconciliation and restoration.
   - By embracing the principles of CRM, religious communities can move beyond the pain of rejection to cultivate cultures of acceptance, belonging, and grace, reflecting the transformative power of love and compassion central to the Christian faith.

Summary

As we journey through the comprehensive framework of the Church Rejection Model, we are reminded of the profound opportunity and responsibility we have as members of religious communities to confront rejection with empathy, humility, and courage. By understanding the root causes, dynamics, and consequences of rejection within the church context, we can work towards healing and renewal, fostering environments where all individuals are welcomed, valued, and embraced as beloved children of God.

Theoretical Foundations of the Church Rejection Model (CRM)

At the heart of the Church Rejection Model (CRM) lies a rich tapestry of theoretical frameworks drawn from psychology, sociology, theology, and pastoral care. These theoretical foundations provide the conceptual underpinnings that guide our understanding of rejection within religious communities and inform our approach to addressing this complex phenomenon. In this chapter, we will delve into the theoretical underpinnings of CRM, exploring key concepts and perspectives from diverse disciplines that shape our understanding of rejection within the church context.

Psychological Theories:
- Attachment Theory: Developed by John Bowlby and Mary Ainsworth, attachment theory explores the ways in which early interpersonal relationships shape individuals' attachment styles and influence their responses to social rejection. Within the context of CRM, attachment theory helps us understand how past experiences of rejection and relational dynamics within religious communities impact individuals' sense of belonging and emotional well-being.
- Social Identity Theory: Proposed by Henri Tajfel and John Turner, social identity theory examines how individuals derive their sense of self from their group memberships and how intergroup dynamics influence behavior and attitudes. Within CRM, social identity theory sheds light on how group norms, social hierarchies, and ingroup/outgroup dynamics contribute to rejection within religious communities.

Sociological Perspectives:
- Structural Functionalism: Rooted in the work of Emile Durkheim, structural functionalism emphasizes the ways in which social institutions contribute to the maintenance of social order and cohesion. Within CRM, structural functionalism helps us understand how religious institutions and communities shape individuals' sense of identity, belonging, and acceptance, as well as the consequences of rejection for social cohesion and collective well-being.
- Conflict Theory: Developed by Karl Marx and further elaborated by scholars such as Max Weber and Ralf Dahrendorf, conflict theory explores the role of power dynamics, inequality, and social conflict in shaping social structures and relationships. Within CRM, conflict theory highlights how power imbalances, cultural norms, and ideological differences contribute to tensions and divisions within religious communities, leading to experiences of rejection and marginalization.

Theological Principles:
- Love and Grace: At the heart of many religious traditions, including Christianity, lie principles of love, grace, and compassion. Within CRM, theological principles inform our understanding of rejection as a departure from these ideals, highlighting the importance of embodying love and grace in our interactions with others and striving towards reconciliation and forgiveness.

- Reconciliation and Restoration: Rooted in Christian theology, the concepts of reconciliation and restoration emphasize the importance of healing relationships, repairing harm, and fostering forgiveness and reconciliation. Within CRM, these theological principles provide a framework for addressing the wounds of rejection and working towards healing and renewal within religious communities.

Conclusion

The theoretical foundations of the Church Rejection Model provide a rich framework for understanding the complexities of rejection within religious communities. By drawing on insights from psychology, sociology, theology, and pastoral care, CRM offers a holistic approach to addressing rejection, informed by a deep understanding of the psychological, social, and spiritual dimensions of human experience. As we continue our exploration of CRM, we will build upon these theoretical foundations to develop practical strategies and interventions for fostering healing, reconciliation, and renewal within religious communities.

CRM Theological Principles

At the heart of many religious traditions lies a profound commitment to love, grace, and reconciliation. These theological principles serve as guiding lights, illuminating the path towards healing, forgiveness, and renewal within the context of faith. In the face of rejection—whether it be social exclusion, judgmental attitudes, or discrimination—these principles offer a beacon of hope, reminding us of the transformative power of love and the possibility of reconciliation even in the midst of pain and division. In this section, we will explore how the theological principles of love, grace, and reconciliation serve as guiding principles for addressing rejection within the context of faith, providing a framework for healing, restoration, and renewal.

1. **Love:** At the core of many religious traditions, including Christianity, is the principle of love—the commandment to love one another as oneself. Love, in this context, is not merely an emotion but a way of being—a radical commitment to empathy, compassion, and selflessness. Within the context of addressing rejection, love challenges us to see beyond our differences, to embrace the inherent worth and dignity of every individual, and to extend grace and compassion to those who have been marginalized or excluded. Love calls us to reach out to the outsider, the outcast, and the marginalized, offering acceptance, understanding, and belonging in the face of rejection.

2. **Grace:** Grace, often described as unmerited favor or divine intervention, lies at the heart of many religious teachings. It is the recognition that none of us are deserving of love or salvation, yet we are granted forgiveness and redemption freely and abundantly. Within the context of addressing rejection, grace reminds us of our own fallibility and the need for humility and compassion in our interactions with others. It invites us to extend forgiveness to those who have hurt us and to seek reconciliation and healing even in the face of pain and injustice. Grace offers the promise of second chances of new beginnings, and of restoration in the midst of brokenness and rejection.

3. **Reconciliation:** Reconciliation is the process of restoring harmony and healing relationships that have been damaged or broken. It is the recognition that, despite our differences and disagreements, we are bound together by a common humanity and a shared desire for peace and wholeness. Within the context of addressing rejection, reconciliation calls us to bridge the divides that separate us, to seek understanding and empathy across lines of difference, and to work towards healing and restoration within our communities of faith. It is a journey of humility, vulnerability, and courage—a journey towards forgiveness, acceptance, and renewal.

Conclusion

The theological principles of love, grace, and reconciliation serve as guiding principles for addressing rejection within the context of faith, providing a framework for healing, restoration, and renewal. In the face of rejection, these principles offer a path towards reconciliation and wholeness, reminding us of the transformative power of love and the possibility of redemption even in the darkest of times. As we navigate the complexities of rejection within our religious communities, may we be guided by these principles, extending love, grace, and reconciliation to all who have been marginalized or excluded.

CRM Key Components

The Church Rejection Model (CRM) offers a comprehensive framework for understanding and addressing the complex phenomenon of rejection within religious communities. Grounded in principles of empathy, inclusivity, and reconciliation, CRM provides a roadmap for navigating the intricate web of factors, dynamics, and consequences that contribute to rejection within the church context. In this chapter, we will explore the key components of CRM, each shedding light on different aspects of rejection and offering insights into how we can foster healing, reconciliation, and renewal within religious communities.

1. **Identification of Rejection Factors:**
   - CRM begins by identifying the key factors that contribute to rejection within religious communities. These factors may include doctrinal differences, social hierarchies, cultural biases, interpersonal conflicts, and systemic injustices.
   - By understanding the root causes of rejection, CRM seeks to address the underlying issues that perpetuate exclusion and division within religious communities, fostering greater awareness, empathy, and understanding among community members.
2. **Formation of Rejection Dynamics:**
   - Rejection within religious communities often manifests through various dynamics such as exclusion from social activities, judgmental attitudes, discrimination, or marginalization.
   - CRM explores how these rejection dynamics arise within the church context, examining the interpersonal and structural factors that contribute to feelings of alienation, loneliness, and unworthiness among community members.
3. **Impact on Individuals and Communities:**
   - Rejection within the church can have profound psychological, emotional, and spiritual consequences for individuals and communities alike. It can erode self-esteem, identity, and sense of belonging, leading to feelings of isolation, despair, and disillusionment.
   - CRM explores the human cost of rejection within religious communities, highlighting the need for greater empathy, support, and healing for those who have been marginalized or excluded.
4. **Interplay of Coping Mechanisms:**
   - Individuals within religious communities employ various coping mechanisms to manage the distress associated with rejection, including seeking social support, engaging in religious practices, or withdrawing from church involvement.
   - CRM examines how these coping mechanisms influence individuals' responses to rejection and their ability to navigate the challenges of belonging and acceptance within religious communities.
5. **Interventions and Strategies for Addressing Rejection:**
   - CRM offers practical interventions and strategies for addressing rejection within religious communities, including education and awareness campaigns, training on inclusivity and empathy, conflict resolution skills, and structural changes to promote greater diversity and inclusion.
   - By implementing evidence-based practices informed by CRM, religious leaders and community members can create environments that promote healing, reconciliation, and renewal for all individuals affected by rejection.

Conclusion

As we explore the key components of the Church Rejection Model, we gain a deeper understanding of the complexities of rejection within religious communities and the pathways towards healing and reconciliation. By addressing the root causes, dynamics, and consequences of rejection, CRM empowers religious communities to cultivate cultures of acceptance, belonging, and grace, reflecting the transformative power of love and compassion central to the teachings of faith.

Key Factors Contributing to Rejection in the Church

In the sacred space of religious communities, where the promise of love, acceptance, and belonging is meant to be most profound, the specter of rejection can cast a long shadow. The Church Rejection Model (CRM) offers a comprehensive framework for understanding the complex dynamics that give rise to rejection within the church context. In this chapter, we will delve into the first key component of CRM: identifying the factors that contribute to rejection within religious communities. By examining doctrinal differences, social hierarchies, cultural biases, and interpersonal conflicts, we gain insight into the multifaceted nature of rejection and lay the groundwork for addressing its root causes.

1. **Doctrinal Differences:**
    - Within religious communities, doctrinal differences can create divisions and tensions that contribute to feelings of rejection. Disagreements over theological interpretations, scriptural teachings, and religious practices can lead to polarization and conflict, undermining the sense of unity and shared purpose within the church.
    - CRM explores how doctrinal differences contribute to rejection within religious communities, examining the ways in which divergent beliefs and interpretations shape individuals' sense of identity, belonging, and acceptance within the faith community.
2. **Social Hierarchies:**
    - Social hierarchies within religious communities can exacerbate feelings of rejection, as individuals vie for status, recognition, and influence within the church context. Whether based on factors such as age, gender, race, or socioeconomic status, hierarchical structures can create barriers to inclusion and participation, perpetuating feelings of marginalization and exclusion.
    - CRM investigates how social hierarchies operate within religious communities, shedding light on the power dynamics and inequalities that shape individuals' experiences of rejection and belonging within the church.
3. **Cultural Biases:**
    - Cultural biases, whether explicit or implicit, can influence perceptions of belonging and acceptance within religious communities. Prejudices based on factors such as ethnicity, nationality, or cultural background can lead to discrimination and marginalization, hindering efforts to create inclusive and welcoming environments within the church.
    - CRM examines how cultural biases contribute to rejection within religious communities, challenging assumptions and stereotypes that undermine the principles of love, acceptance, and inclusivity central to many faith traditions.

4. **Interpersonal Conflicts:**
   - Interpersonal conflicts, whether between individuals or within groups, can disrupt the harmony and cohesion of religious communities, leading to feelings of rejection and alienation among community members. Whether stemming from differences in personality, values, or priorities, conflicts can create divisions that undermine the sense of unity and fellowship within the church.
   - CRM explores the dynamics of interpersonal conflicts within religious communities, offering insights into the underlying causes and consequences of conflict and highlighting strategies for fostering reconciliation and healing within the faith community.

Conclusion

As we examine the key factors contributing to rejection within the church, we gain a deeper understanding of the complexities of this phenomenon and the challenges it poses for religious communities. By identifying doctrinal differences, social hierarchies, cultural biases, and interpersonal conflicts, CRM lays the groundwork for addressing the root causes of rejection and fostering greater empathy, understanding, and reconciliation within the church context. Through thoughtful reflection and dialogue, religious communities can begin to confront the forces of rejection and work towards creating environments that reflect the values of love, acceptance, and inclusivity central to their faith traditions.

Church Rejection Key Factors

Within the sacred confines of religious communities, where the ideals of love, acceptance, and unity are espoused, the reality of rejection can cast a shadow over the hearts of believers. In the context of the church, rejection often stems from a complex interplay of factors that shape the dynamics of belonging and exclusion within the faith community. Understanding these key factors is essential for unraveling the complexities of rejection and fostering environments of inclusivity, empathy, and reconciliation within religious communities.

In this section, we will explore the key factors that contribute to rejection in the church, shedding light on the doctrinal differences, social hierarchies, cultural biases, and interpersonal conflicts that underpin this pervasive phenomenon. By examining these factors through the lens of real-world examples and theoretical insights, we aim to deepen our understanding of rejection within the church context and identify pathways towards healing, renewal, and transformation.

As we embark on this exploration, let us hold in our hearts the hope and conviction that, even in the face of rejection, the principles of love, grace, and reconciliation that lie at the heart of our faith traditions can guide us towards greater understanding, compassion, and unity within the body of Christ.

Consider a hypothetical scenario in which a new member, Maria, joins a conservative religious congregation. Maria, who comes from a more liberal background, holds progressive views on social issues such as LGBTQ+ rights and gender equality. However, within the congregation, there exists a doctrinal stance that opposes such views, promoting traditional interpretations of scripture.

1. **Doctrinal Differences:** Maria's progressive beliefs clash with the conservative doctrinal stance of the congregation. Despite her genuine desire to connect with her fellow church members and participate in communal worship, Maria finds herself at odds with the prevailing theological perspectives. Conversations on sensitive topics such as gender roles or marriage equality often lead to discomfort and tension, as Maria's viewpoints are perceived as challenging or even undermining the church's teachings.
2. **Social Hierarchies:** Within the congregation, there exists a clear social hierarchy based on adherence to traditional beliefs and practices. Those who align closely with the established doctrines hold positions of influence and leadership within the church, while individuals like Maria, who hold differing views, find themselves on the margins of the community. Despite her efforts to engage and contribute positively, Maria encounters subtle forms of exclusion and marginalization, as her perspectives are deemed less valid or acceptable within the social hierarchy of the congregation.
3. **Cultural Biases:** The congregation's conservative doctrinal stance reflects broader cultural biases prevalent within the community. Traditional gender roles, heteronormative assumptions, and conservative values shape the collective mindset of the congregation, influencing perceptions of acceptability and belonging. As a result, Maria's progressive beliefs are met with skepticism and resistance, as they challenge deeply ingrained cultural norms and expectations within the church community.
4. **Interpersonal Conflicts:** Maria's presence within the congregation sparks interpersonal conflicts and tensions among church members. Conversations around divisive issues often escalate into heated debates and disagreements, as individuals with differing viewpoints struggle to find common ground. Despite Maria's efforts to foster understanding and dialogue, she finds herself caught in the

crossfire of interpersonal conflicts, feeling increasingly isolated and rejected by her fellow church members.

In this example, the key factors contributing to rejection within the church—doctrinal differences, social hierarchies, cultural biases, and interpersonal conflicts—converge to create a challenging and unwelcoming environment for Maria. Despite her sincere desire to connect with her faith community, Maria faces barriers to acceptance and belonging due to the prevailing dynamics of rejection within the congregation.

Rejection Scenario

This section focuses on navigating differences in beliefs and values within religious communities, using the scenario of Maria's experience as a focal point. In this section, we will explore the challenges and opportunities that arise when individuals with differing beliefs and perspectives come together within a religious congregation. Maria, a new member with progressive views on social issues, finds herself navigating the doctrinal stance of a conservative religious congregation. Through a series of reflective questions and exercises, we will delve into Maria's experience and consider strategies for fostering understanding, acceptance, and unity within diverse faith communities. Join us as we embark on a journey of exploration and reflection, seeking insights that can enrich our understanding of the complexities of belief and belonging within religious contexts.

CRM Rejection Reflection

1. Reflect on Maria's situation. How do you think she feels about joining a conservative religious congregation with opposing views to her own?

2. Imagine you are Maria. How would you navigate the tension between your own beliefs and the doctrinal stance of the congregation?

3. Brainstorm potential coping mechanisms Maria could employ to deal with the challenges of being in a religious community with opposing views.

4. What are some potential sources of support for Maria within the congregation? How might she go about seeking support from fellow church members or church leadership?

5. Consider Maria's potential role within the congregation. How might her progressive views contribute to discussions and debates within the church community?

6. Imagine you are a member of the church leadership. How would you address the tension between Maria's progressive views and the congregation's doctrinal stance?

7. Reflect on the importance of fostering inclusivity and understanding within religious communities. What steps could the congregation take to create a more welcoming environment for individuals with diverse perspectives?

Church Rejection Model Dynamics

Within the intricate tapestry of religious communities, rejection can manifest through complex dynamics that shape interactions and relationships among members. Understanding the formation of these rejection dynamics is crucial for unraveling the root causes of exclusion and fostering environments of acceptance and belonging within the church. In this chapter, we will delve into the formation of church rejection dynamics, exploring the interpersonal and structural factors that contribute to feelings of rejection and alienation among community members. Through careful examination and reflection, we will gain insight into the underlying mechanisms that perpetuate exclusion within religious communities and identify strategies for fostering greater empathy, understanding, and reconciliation. delve into how CRM explores the multifaceted dynamics that give rise to rejection within church settings, including exclusion from social activities, judgmental attitudes, discrimination, and marginalization. By examining these dynamics through the lens of CRM, we aim to uncover the underlying factors and mechanisms that perpetuate feelings of rejection and alienation among community members. Through reflection and analysis, we will gain insight into how these rejection dynamics form and evolve within religious communities, laying the groundwork for fostering environments of inclusivity, empathy, and reconciliation within the church. Join us on this journey as we unravel the complexities of rejection dynamics and explore pathways towards greater understanding and acceptance within religious communities.

In the diverse landscape of religious communities, church rejection can manifest in various forms, shaping the experiences and interactions of individuals within different church settings. From traditional churches to contemporary megachurches, each environment presents unique dynamics that can contribute to feelings of exclusion and alienation among community members. In this section, we will explore how church rejection manifests in each of the following settings, shedding light on the diverse dynamics of exclusion, judgment, discrimination, and marginalization that individuals may encounter within the sacred halls of the church. Through reflection and analysis, we aim to deepen our understanding of the complexities of rejection within religious communities and identify pathways towards greater empathy, understanding, and reconciliation within the church. Join us as we embark on a journey of exploration and reflection, seeking to unravel the intricacies of rejection dynamics and cultivate spaces of belonging and acceptance within the sacred spaces of the church.

The Church Rejection Model (CRM) manifests within different church settings through various dynamics such as exclusion from social activities, judgmental attitudes, discrimination, or marginalization:

1. **Traditional Churches:**
   - In traditional church settings, rejection dynamics may manifest through exclusion from social activities such as fellowship groups, potlucks, or community events. Individuals who do not conform to traditional norms or beliefs may find themselves marginalized and excluded from these communal gatherings.
   - Judgmental attitudes within traditional churches can contribute to feelings of rejection among members who hold differing viewpoints or lifestyles. Those who deviate from the perceived norms of the church may face criticism or ostracism from their peers.
   - Discrimination based on factors such as race, gender, or sexual orientation can also occur within traditional church settings, leading to the marginalization of minority groups and the perpetuation of harmful stereotypes and prejudices.

2. **Contemporary Churches:**
   - In contemporary church settings, rejection dynamics may manifest through exclusion from social activities that cater to specific demographics or interests. Individuals who do not fit the mold of the "typical" churchgoer may feel overlooked or sidelined in these settings.
   - Judgmental attitudes within contemporary churches can arise from pressure to conform to certain standards of behavior or appearance. Those who do not meet these expectations may face criticism or disapproval from their peers.
   - Discrimination based on factors such as socio-economic status or educational background can also occur within contemporary church settings, perpetuating divides between different segments of the congregation and hindering efforts to foster inclusivity and unity.

3. **Megachurches:**
   - In megachurch settings, rejection dynamics may manifest through exclusion from social activities that cater to specific affinity groups or ministries within the church. Individuals who do not fit into these niche groups may struggle to find a sense of belonging and connection within the larger congregation.
   - Judgmental attitudes within megachurches can arise from pressure to conform to the charismatic leadership or dominant culture of the church. Those who do not align with the prevailing values or beliefs may feel marginalized or overlooked in these settings.
   - Discrimination based on factors such as age or marital status can also occur within megachurch settings, as certain demographics may be prioritized or favored over others in terms of leadership opportunities or involvement in church activities.

4. **Small Community Churches:**
   - In small community church settings, rejection dynamics may manifest through exclusion from social activities that are centered around tight-knit groups or cliques within the congregation. Individuals who are not part of these inner circles may struggle to find acceptance and connection within the community.
   - Judgmental attitudes within small community churches can arise from close-knit relationships and interpersonal dynamics. Gossip, rumors, and cliquish behavior may contribute to feelings of rejection and isolation among certain members.
   - Discrimination based on factors such as family background or personal history can also occur within small community church settings, as longstanding feuds or rivalries may impact interpersonal relationships and interactions within the congregation.

Overall, the manifestation of rejection dynamics within different church settings highlights the need for intentional efforts to foster environments of inclusivity, empathy, and reconciliation within religious communities. By recognizing and addressing these dynamics with humility, compassion, and grace, church leaders and members can work towards creating spaces of belonging and acceptance for all individuals, regardless of their background, beliefs, or circumstances.

Church Dynamics of Rejection Interpersonal and Structural

Within the intricate fabric of religious communities, church rejection can manifest through a complex interplay of interpersonal and structural dynamics. These dynamics shape the relationships, interactions, and power structures within the church, influencing the experiences of individuals and groups within the community. In this section, we embark on an exploration of the interpersonal and structural dynamics of church rejection, delving into the subtle nuances and underlying mechanisms that contribute to feelings of exclusion, alienation, and marginalization. Through careful examination and analysis, we seek to uncover the root causes of rejection within religious communities and identify strategies for fostering environments of inclusivity, empathy, and reconciliation within the sacred spaces of the church. Join us as we navigate the intricate webs of interpersonal and structural dynamics, seeking to unravel the complexities of rejection and cultivate spaces of belonging and acceptance within the body of Christ.

What are Interpersonal and Structural Church Dynamics of Church Rejection?

Interpersonal Church Dynamics

Interpersonal dynamics of rejection within the church refer to the relational interactions and behaviors among individuals that contribute to feelings of exclusion, alienation, or marginalization. This includes phenomena such as cliques, gossip, judgmental attitudes, and a lack of empathy or understanding towards others' experiences.

Structural Church Dynamics

Structural dynamics of rejection within the church pertain to the organizational and systemic factors that perpetuate exclusion and marginalization within the community. This encompasses hierarchical power structures, lack of diversity and representation in leadership, inequitable resource distribution, and rigid organizational policies or procedures that create barriers to inclusion and participation for certain individuals.

The interpersonal and structural dynamics of church rejection interact and reinforce each other, creating complex and multifaceted experiences of exclusion and alienation within religious communities. Recognizing and addressing these dynamics is essential for fostering environments of inclusivity, empathy, and belonging within the church. This chart provides a clear comparison between the interpersonal and structural dynamics of church rejection, highlighting their distinct characteristics and areas of influence within religious communities.

Aspect	Interpersonal Dynamics	Structural Dynamics
Focus	Relational interactions among individuals	Organizational and systemic factors
Examples	Cliques, gossip, judgmental attitudes	Hierarchical power structures, lack of diversity in leadership, inequitable resource distribution
Influence	Individual attitudes and behaviors	Institutional norms, practices, and policies
Impact	Immediate and direct on individuals	Long-term and systemic effects
Addressing	Addressed through interpersonal communication and relationship-building	Addressed through structural changes, policy revisions, and institutional reform

Interpersonal Church Dynamics Examples

- **Cliques and Exclusionary Groups:**
    - Within church communities, cliques and exclusive social groups can form, creating barriers to inclusion for certain individuals. Those who do not belong to these cliques may feel marginalized and excluded from key social interactions and events.
- **Gossip and Rumors:**
    - Gossip and rumors can spread quickly within church settings, leading to the ostracism and alienation of individuals targeted by such behavior. False or exaggerated information can damage reputations and relationships, fostering an environment of distrust and suspicion.
- **Judgmental Attitudes:**
    - Judgmental attitudes towards others' beliefs, behaviors, or lifestyles can contribute to feelings of rejection within church communities. Individuals may feel criticized or condemned for deviating from perceived norms, leading to a sense of alienation and unworthiness.
- **Lack of Empathy and Understanding:**
    - A lack of empathy and understanding towards individuals facing personal challenges or struggles can exacerbate feelings of rejection within church communities. Those in need of support may feel ignored or dismissed, further isolating them from the community.
- **Relational Interactions:**
    - Interpersonal dynamics involve the direct interactions and relationships among individuals within the church community.
- **Behavior and Attitudes:**
    - These dynamics encompass behaviors such as cliques, gossip, judgmental attitudes, and a lack of empathy towards others' experiences.
- **Individual-Level Factors:**
    - Interpersonal dynamics are influenced by individual attitudes, beliefs, and behaviors, and can vary widely based on personal interactions and relationships.
- **Immediate Impact:**
    - Interpersonal dynamics can have an immediate and direct impact on individuals' feelings of exclusion, alienation, or marginalization within the church community. Examples of interpersonal dynamics include exclusion from social groups, gossip or rumors about individuals, criticism or judgment from peers, and lack of empathy towards others' struggles.

Structural Church Dynamics Examples

- **Hierarchical Power Structures:**
    - Church communities often have hierarchical power structures, with clergy or church leaders holding significant authority and influence. The concentration of power in the hands of a few can lead to feelings of exclusion among those who are not part of the leadership circle.
- **Lack of Diversity and Representation:**
    - Homogeneity within church leadership and decision-making bodies can perpetuate feelings of exclusion among minority groups within the congregation. The absence of diverse voices and perspectives may leave certain individuals feeling marginalized and unheard.
- **Inequitable Resource Distribution:**
    - Inequitable distribution of resources such as funding, facilities, or opportunities for involvement can contribute to feelings of rejection within church communities. Those who are not prioritized or included in resource allocation decisions may feel undervalued and overlooked.
- **Rigid Organizational Policies:**
    - Rigid organizational policies and procedures can create barriers to inclusion and participation for certain individuals within church communities. Requirements for membership, leadership roles, or involvement in church activities may be exclusionary or prohibitive for some members of the congregation.
- **Organizational Factors:**
    - Structural dynamics involve the broader organizational and systemic factors within the church community that perpetuate exclusion and marginalization.
- **Systemic Inequities:**
    - These dynamics encompass hierarchical power structures, lack of diversity and representation in leadership, inequitable resource distribution, and rigid organizational policies or procedures.
- **Institutional-Level Factors:**
    - Structural dynamics are influenced by institutional norms, practices, and policies that shape the overall functioning of the church community.
- **Long-Term Impact:**
    - Structural dynamics can have long-term and systemic effects on individuals' sense of belonging and inclusion within the church, impacting their opportunities for participation and engagement. Examples: Examples of structural dynamics include unequal representation of minority groups in leadership roles, limited access to resources or opportunities for certain members, exclusionary policies or practices, and entrenched power imbalances within the church hierarchy.

Summary

In summary, interpersonal dynamics of church rejection involve direct interactions and relationships among individuals, while structural dynamics pertain to broader organizational and systemic factors within the church community. While interpersonal dynamics focus on individual-level behaviors and attitudes, structural dynamics address institutional-level inequities and power dynamics that perpetuate exclusion and marginalization.

Church Rejection Model Hidden Biases and Power Imbalances

In the exploration of church rejection, it is essential to confront the hidden biases and power imbalances that perpetuate exclusion and marginalization within religious communities. While the Church Rejection Model (CRM) offers a framework for understanding rejection dynamics, it is not immune to the influence of societal prejudices, systemic inequities, and individual biases. In this chapter, we will delve into the hidden biases and power imbalances that underpin church rejection, shedding light on the ways in which they shape interpersonal interactions, organizational structures, and communal attitudes within the church. By uncovering these biases and imbalances, we can begin to address the root causes of rejection and work towards fostering environments of inclusivity, equity, and belonging within religious communities.

Hidden Biases:

1. **Implicit Biases:** Implicit biases are unconscious attitudes or stereotypes that influence our perceptions and behaviors towards others. Within the church, implicit biases may manifest in subtle ways, such as assumptions about individuals' backgrounds, beliefs, or identities based on superficial characteristics.
2. **Cultural Biases:** Cultural biases refer to the societal norms, values, and beliefs that shape our understanding of acceptable behavior and social interactions. In the context of church rejection, cultural biases may lead to the marginalization of certain groups within the congregation, perpetuating stereotypes and prejudices based on race, gender, sexuality, or socioeconomic status.
3. **Confirmation Bias:** Confirmation bias is the tendency to seek out information that confirms our existing beliefs or prejudices while ignoring or discounting evidence that contradicts them. Within religious communities, confirmation bias may lead to the reinforcement of exclusionary attitudes or practices towards individuals who deviate from perceived norms or doctrines.
4. **Halo Effect:** The halo effect is the tendency to attribute positive qualities to individuals based on one favorable trait or characteristic. In the church context, the halo effect may result in the privilege of certain individuals or groups within the congregation, while others are overlooked or undervalued.

Power Imbalances:

1. Hierarchical Structures: Many religious communities have hierarchical structures of authority, with clergy or church leaders holding significant power and influence. These hierarchical structures can create power imbalances that privilege certain individuals or groups within the congregation while marginalizing others.
2. Gender and Leadership: Gender norms and stereotypes may influence perceptions of leadership suitability within the church, leading to the underrepresentation of women or non-binary individuals in leadership roles. This gender imbalance perpetuates power differentials that contribute to feelings of exclusion and inequality within the congregation.
3. Socioeconomic Disparities: Socioeconomic disparities within the church community can create power imbalances that impact individuals' access to resources, opportunities, and decision-making processes. Those with greater financial resources or social capital may wield disproportionate influence within the congregation, while others are marginalized or disenfranchised.
4. Institutional Policies and Practices: Institutional policies and practices within the church may reinforce power imbalances by favoring certain groups or individuals over others. Discriminatory policies, lack of transparency, and unequal treatment can exacerbate feelings of exclusion and marginalization among those who are not part of the dominant power structure.

In confronting the hidden biases and power imbalances that perpetuate church rejection, we must acknowledge the role that these factors play in shaping the experiences of individuals within religious communities. By uncovering and addressing these biases and imbalances, we can work towards creating environments of inclusivity, equity, and justice within the church, where all members are valued, respected, and empowered to fully participate in the life of the congregation. This chart provides examples of how hidden biases and power imbalances can manifest within the Church Rejection Model, influencing perceptions, behaviors, and organizational structures within religious communities.

Aspect	Hidden Biases Examples	Power Imbalances Examples
Implicit Biases	Assuming individuals of a certain race or ethnicity are less spiritually mature or committed based on stereotypes.	Clergy predominantly consisting of individuals from a specific demographic group, leading to a lack of diverse perspectives and experiences in leadership positions.
Cultural Biases	Expecting individuals to conform to specific gender roles or expressions within the church community.	Women or LGBTQ+ individuals being excluded from leadership roles or marginalized within the congregation due to adherence to traditional gender norms.
Confirmation Bias	Seeking out evidence that supports preconceived notions about certain theological beliefs or practices, while dismissing contradictory viewpoints.	Prioritizing the perspectives and experiences of individuals who align with the dominant theological or doctrinal framework, while disregarding alternative interpretations or perspectives.
Halo Effect	Assuming that individuals who hold positions of authority or leadership within the church are inherently virtuous or righteous in all aspects of their character and decision-making.	Granting preferential treatment or undue influence to individuals in leadership roles, based solely on their perceived spiritual stature or authority.

CRM Rejection Reflection

1. Reflect on your own experiences within the church community. Have you ever observed or experienced hidden biases or power imbalances that perpetuate feelings of rejection or exclusion?

2. Consider the impact of hidden biases and power imbalances on individuals within the church. How might these dynamics affect one's sense of belonging, worthiness, and spiritual well-being?

3. Examine the role of leadership within the church in addressing hidden biases and power imbalances. What steps can church leaders take to promote inclusivity, equity, and justice within the congregation?

4. Consider the role of accountability and transparency in addressing power imbalances within the church. How can accountability structures be implemented to ensure fair treatment and representation for all members of the congregation?

5. Reflect on the intersectionality of hidden biases and power imbalances within the church. How do factors such as race, gender, sexuality, and socio-economic status intersect to shape experiences of rejection and exclusion?

6. Consider the role of education and awareness-raising in addressing hidden biases and power imbalances. How can church members and leaders engage in ongoing education and dialogue to promote understanding and empathy within the congregation?

7. Reflect on your own responsibility as a member of the church community to address hidden biases and power imbalances. What steps can you take to contribute to a more inclusive, equitable, and compassionate church environment?

CRM Psychological, Emotional, and Spiritual Consequences

In the realm of religious communities, rejection can have profound psychological, emotional, and spiritual consequences for individuals who experience it. The Church Rejection Model (CRM) offers a framework for understanding and examining these multifaceted impacts within the context of the church. By exploring the psychological, emotional, and spiritual dimensions of rejection, CRM provides insights into the complexities of human experience and the profound effects of interpersonal dynamics and structural factors within religious communities. In this section, we delve into how CRM examines the psychological, emotional, and spiritual consequences of rejection within the church, shedding light on the ways in which rejection can affect individuals' well-being, sense of identity, and relationship with their faith. Through careful examination and reflection, we aim to deepen our understanding of the far-reaching effects of rejection and identify strategies for fostering healing, resilience, and reconciliation within religious communities. Join us as we explore the intersection of psychology, emotion, and spirituality within the context of church rejection, seeking to cultivate spaces of understanding, empathy, and restoration within the sacred spaces of the church.

Church Rejection Psychological Impact

Church rejection can have significant psychological impacts on individuals, affecting their mental health, emotional well-being, and sense of self-worth. Some of the psychological impacts of church rejection may include:

- **Low Self-Esteem**: Rejection from the church community can lead to feelings of inadequacy, self-doubt, and low self-esteem. Individuals may internalize the rejection as a reflection of their own worthiness, leading to a diminished sense of self-value.
- **Depression and Anxiety**: Church rejection can trigger symptoms of depression and anxiety, including sadness, hopelessness, and worry. The loss of social support and community connection that often accompanies rejection can exacerbate feelings of loneliness and isolation, contributing to mental health struggles.
- **Identity Confusion**: For many people, religious identity is closely intertwined with their sense of self. Church rejection can create confusion and turmoil around one's identity, causing individuals to question their beliefs, values, and sense of belonging within the faith community.
- **Spiritual Struggles**: Church rejection can shake individuals' faith and trust in their religious beliefs and practices. Feelings of betrayal, disillusionment, and anger towards God or spiritual leaders may arise, leading to spiritual crises and existential questioning.
- **Social Withdrawal**: Individuals who experience church rejection may withdraw from social interactions and community involvement, fearing further rejection or judgment from others. This social withdrawal can exacerbate feelings of loneliness and exacerbate mental health challenges.
- **Emotional Distress**: Church rejection often elicits a range of intense emotions, including sadness, anger, shame, and grief. These emotional responses may be prolonged and difficult to manage, impacting individuals' overall emotional well-being and quality of life.
- **Coping Strategies**: Individuals may develop maladaptive coping strategies, such as substance abuse, self-harm, or disordered eating, in an attempt to numb or escape from the pain of rejection. These coping mechanisms can further exacerbate psychological distress and lead to additional health concerns.
- **Impact on Relationships**: Church rejection can strain relationships with family members, friends, and other social supporters who may be part of the same religious community. Conflict and tension may arise as individuals navigate their experiences of rejection and seek support from others.

Overall, the psychological impacts of church rejection are profound and multifaceted, affecting individuals' mental health, emotional well-being, and sense of identity. It is essential for individuals experiencing church rejection to seek support from trusted loved ones, mental health professionals, or spiritual advisors to navigate these challenges and promote healing and resilience.

Church Rejection Psychological Impact Definitions

Let's define each of the psychological impacts of church rejection:

1. **Low Self-Esteem**: Low self-esteem refers to a negative perception of oneself and a diminished sense of self-worth. In the context of church rejection, individuals may internalize feelings of inadequacy and inferiority, leading to a negative self-image and reduced confidence in their abilities and value as a person.
2. **Depression and Anxiety**: Depression is a mood disorder characterized by persistent feelings of sadness, hopelessness, and loss of interest or pleasure in activities. Anxiety is a condition characterized by excessive worry, fear, and apprehension. Church rejection can trigger symptoms of depression and anxiety, exacerbating existing mental health conditions or precipitating the onset of new ones.
3. **Identity Confusion**: Identity confusion refers to a state of uncertainty or conflict regarding one's sense of self, including beliefs, values, and personal characteristics. Church rejection can challenge individuals' religious identity, causing them to question their beliefs, values, and sense of belonging within the faith community.
4. **Spiritual Struggles**: Spiritual struggles involve existential questioning, doubt, and distress related to one's faith or spirituality. Church rejection can shake individuals' faith and trust in their religious beliefs and practices, leading to spiritual crises and existential uncertainty.
5. **Social Withdrawal**: Social withdrawal refers to a pattern of avoiding or limiting social interactions and activities. Church rejection may cause individuals to withdraw from social connections and community involvement, fearing further rejection or judgment from others.
6. **Emotional Distress**: Emotional distress encompasses a range of intense emotions, including sadness, anger, shame, and grief. Church rejection can elicit these strong emotional responses, which may be prolonged and difficult to manage, impacting individuals' overall emotional well-being and quality of life.
7. **Maladaptive Coping Strategies**: Maladaptive coping strategies are unhealthy or ineffective ways of managing stress and emotional distress. In response to church rejection, individuals may turn to substance abuse, self-harm, or disordered eating as a means of numbing or escaping from their pain.
8. **Impact on Relationships**: Church rejection can strain relationships with family members, friends, and other social supports who may be part of the same religious community. Conflict and tension may arise as individuals navigate their experiences of rejection and seek support from others.

These psychological impacts of church rejection are multifaceted and can have profound effects on individuals' mental health, emotional well-being, and sense of identity. It is essential for individuals experiencing church rejection to seek support from trusted loved ones, mental health professionals, or spiritual advisors to navigate these challenges and promote healing and resilience.

Church Rejection Psychological Scenarios

The psychological impacts of church rejection delve deep into the core of individuals' mental and emotional well-being, often leaving lasting scars on their sense of identity and spiritual resilience. When individuals experience rejection within their religious community, the repercussions extend far beyond mere social exclusion. They touch upon fundamental aspects of self-esteem, emotional stability, and spiritual belief systems. In this section, we explore the profound psychological impacts of church rejection, shedding light on the intricate interplay between rejection and mental health. Through examination and example, we seek to understand how rejection within the church can shape individuals' perceptions of themselves, their relationships, and their faith.

Scenario I: Devoted Church Member

Consider Sarah, a devoted member of her church community for many years. Sarah actively participated in church activities, formed close friendships within the congregation, and found solace and support in her faith. However, as Sarah began to openly express her doubts and questions about certain theological teachings, she noticed a shift in her relationships with fellow church members. She was met with skepticism, criticism, and ultimately exclusion from certain social circles within the church. Despite her sincere desire to engage in meaningful dialogue and exploration of her faith, Sarah felt increasingly isolated and rejected by those whom she once considered her spiritual family.

As a result of the rejection she experienced, Sarah's self-esteem plummeted, and she began to question her worthiness and value as a person. She struggled with feelings of sadness, anxiety, and loneliness, finding it challenging to trust others or form new relationships outside of the church community. Sarah's faith, once a source of strength and comfort, now felt shaky and uncertain, as she grappled with doubts and spiritual disillusionment.

In this example, we see how church rejection can have profound psychological impacts on individuals like Sarah, affecting their self-esteem, emotional well-being, and sense of spiritual identity. Sarah's experience highlights the complexities of navigating rejection within the church and underscores the need for compassionate support and understanding within religious communities.

The psychological impact of church rejection can be especially poignant for individuals grappling with spiritual struggles within their faith community. When individuals experiencing doubts, questioning, or crisis of faith are met with rejection or judgment from their religious community, the consequences can be deeply distressing and profound. In this section, we explore the unique psychological impacts of church rejection on those dealing with spiritual struggles, examining how rejection can exacerbate feelings of doubt, isolation, and existential angst. Through analysis and example, we aim to shed light on the complex interplay between rejection and spiritual well-being, and the importance of compassion and understanding within religious communities.

Scenario II: Church Member

Meet John, a devout member of his church who has always found solace and guidance in his faith. However, in recent months, John has been grappling with doubts and questions about fundamental aspects of his religious beliefs. He finds himself wrestling with theological concepts, struggling to reconcile his faith with his evolving understanding of the world. Seeking support and guidance, John turns to his church community, hoping to engage in meaningful dialogue and exploration of his spiritual journey.

However, instead of receiving the understanding and empathy he had hoped for, John is met with skepticism, criticism, and rejection from some members of his church. He is told that his doubts are a sign of weak faith and lack of commitment, and that he should simply "pray harder" or "trust in God's plan." Feeling misunderstood and alienated, John begins to withdraw from his church community, fearing further judgment and condemnation.

As a result of the rejection he experiences, John's spiritual struggles intensify, and he finds himself engulfed in feelings of doubt, confusion, and existential angst. He questions his place within the church and wonders if he will ever find the support and understanding he so desperately seeks. John's once vibrant faith now feels fragile and uncertain, as he grapples with the profound psychological impacts of rejection within his religious community.

In this example, we see how church rejection can exacerbate the psychological challenges faced by individuals like John, who are dealing with spiritual struggles within their faith community. John's experience underscores the importance of compassion, empathy, and acceptance within religious communities, particularly when individuals are navigating complex questions of faith and belief.

The psychological impact of church rejection can be particularly profound for women within religious communities. When women experience rejection based on gender, whether through exclusion from leadership roles, dismissal of their voices, or judgment of their choices, the consequences can deeply affect their sense of self-worth, identity, and spiritual well-being. In this section, we explore the psychological impacts of church rejection on women, examining how gender-based rejection can exacerbate feelings of inadequacy, powerlessness, and alienation. Through analysis and example, we aim to shed light on the unique challenges faced by women within religious communities and the importance of fostering inclusivity, empowerment, and support within the church.

Scenario III: Church Member

Consider Sarah, a devout member of her church who has long felt called to serve in leadership roles within her congregation. Sarah is passionate about using her gifts and talents to contribute to the church community and feels a deep sense of purpose in serving others. However, despite her qualifications, dedication, and enthusiasm, Sarah finds herself repeatedly overlooked for leadership positions within the church.

Instead, she sees men with less experience and qualifications being appointed to leadership roles, while women like her are relegated to supporting roles or dismissed altogether. Feeling marginalized and undervalued, Sarah begins to question her worthiness and abilities, wondering if her gender will always be a barrier to achieving her aspirations within the church.

As a result of the rejection, she experiences, Sarah's confidence and self-esteem begin to erode, and she struggles with feelings of frustration, anger, and disillusionment. She finds it increasingly difficult to connect with her faith community, feeling like her voice and contributions are not valued or respected. Sarah's once vibrant spiritual life now feels tainted by the sting of rejection, as she grapples with the psychological toll of gender-based exclusion within her religious community.

In this example, we see how church rejection can exacerbate the psychological challenges faced by women like Sarah, who are dealing with gender-based discrimination within their faith community. Sarah's experience underscores the importance of addressing gender inequality and fostering inclusivity, empowerment, and support for women within the church.

The psychological impact of church rejection can be uniquely profound for individuals in leadership positions within religious communities, such as pastors' wives. As integral members of the church community, pastors' wives often face heightened expectations, scrutiny, and pressures to conform to certain roles and expectations. When pastors' wives experience rejection within their church community, whether through gossip, criticism, or exclusion, the consequences can deeply affect their mental and emotional well-being, as well as their sense of identity and purpose. In this section, we explore the psychological impacts of church rejection on pastors' wives, examining how rejection can exacerbate feelings of isolation, inadequacy, and disillusionment. Through analysis and example, we aim to shed light on the unique challenges faced by pastors' wives within religious communities and the importance of providing support, understanding, and compassion within the church.

Scenario III: Pastor Wife

Meet Emily, the wife of a pastor in a vibrant and close-knit church community. Emily has always been deeply committed to supporting her husband's ministry and serving alongside him in various church activities. However, despite her dedication and tireless efforts, Emily begins to notice subtle signs of rejection and exclusion from some members of the congregation.

She overhears whispers and gossip about her appearance, her parenting style, and even her role within the church. She is excluded from important decision-making processes and leadership discussions, despite her desire to contribute and be involved. Feeling increasingly isolated and marginalized, Emily struggles to maintain her sense of confidence and belonging within the church community.

As a result of the rejection she experiences, Emily's mental and emotional well-being begins to suffer. She grapples with feelings of inadequacy, self-doubt, and loneliness, wondering if she will ever be fully accepted and valued within her church community. The once vibrant and fulfilling aspects of her role as a pastor's wife now feel tainted by the sting of rejection, as she navigates the psychological toll of exclusion and judgment within her religious community.

In this example, we see how church rejection can have a profound psychological impact on pastors' wives like Emily, who are navigating the complexities of leadership and service within their church community. Emily's experience underscores the importance of recognizing and addressing the unique challenges faced by pastors' wives and providing them with support, understanding, and affirmation within the church.

The psychological impact of church rejection can reverberate through various aspects of religious community life, including involvement in church activities such as choir participation. For individuals who pour their hearts and talents into contributing to the worship experience, rejection within the church can be deeply distressing and disruptive. Choir members, in particular, often form close bonds with fellow singers and invest significant time and energy into their musical ministry. When these individuals experience rejection, whether through exclusion from performances, criticism of their abilities, or interpersonal conflicts, the consequences can profoundly affect their mental and emotional well-being. In this section, we explore the psychological impacts of church rejection on choir members, examining how rejection can exacerbate feelings of inadequacy, shame, and disconnection. Through analysis and example, we aim to shed light on the unique challenges faced by choir members within religious communities and the importance of fostering support, acceptance, and appreciation within the church.

Scenario IV: Choir Member

Meet David, a dedicated member of the church choir who has sung in the choir for many years. David has always found great joy and fulfillment in using his musical talents to praise and worship alongside his fellow choir members. However, in recent months, David begins to notice a shift in the dynamics within the choir.

He is excluded from solo opportunities and special performances, despite his years of faithful service and vocal skill. He receives subtle criticisms from choir leaders about his singing technique and is made to feel unworthy and inadequate compared to other members. Feeling increasingly isolated and undervalued, David's once joyful participation in the choir begins to feel like a burden.

As a result of the rejection he experiences, David's confidence and self-esteem begin to wane, and he struggles with feelings of shame and self-doubt. He questions whether his talents are truly appreciated or valued within the church community and finds it increasingly difficult to connect with his fellow choir members. David's once vibrant passion for music and worship now feels tainted by the sting of rejection, as he navigates the psychological toll of exclusion and criticism within his religious community.

In this example, we see how church rejection can have a profound psychological impact on choir members like David, who invest their time, talent, and passion into serving within their church community. David's experience underscores the importance of recognizing and valuing the contributions of choir members and providing them with support, affirmation, and appreciation within the church.

Summary

The psychological impact of church rejection is far-reaching and deeply personal, touching upon fundamental aspects of individuals' mental and emotional well-being. Whether experienced by pastors' wives, choir members, or individuals grappling with spiritual struggles, rejection within the church community can exacerbate feelings of inadequacy, shame, and disconnection. Through the scenarios of Emily, the pastor's wife, and David, the choir member, we have witnessed the profound toll that rejection can take on individuals who pour their hearts and talents into serving and participating within their religious communities. These examples highlight the importance of recognizing and addressing the unique challenges faced by individuals within the church, as well as the need for fostering support, acceptance, and appreciation within religious communities. By acknowledging the psychological impacts of church rejection and working towards creating environments of understanding, empathy, and inclusion, we can strive towards healing, resilience, and reconciliation within the sacred spaces of the church.

Church Rejection
Emotional Impact

Emotional church rejection refers to the experience of feeling excluded, dismissed, or invalidated within one's religious community, leading to emotional distress, hurt, and disillusionment. It involves the perception of being unwelcome, unaccepted, or marginalized by fellow congregants, church leaders, or the religious institution itself. Emotional church rejection can manifest in various forms, such as being ignored or shunned, criticized or judged, or denied opportunities for participation or involvement within the church community. It can deeply impact individuals' emotional well-being, sense of belonging, and relationship with their faith, often triggering feelings of hurt, disappointment, betrayal, isolation, and self-doubt. Recognizing and addressing emotional church rejection is essential for fostering inclusivity, empathy, and support within religious communities, promoting healing, resilience, and reconciliation among those affected.

Church Rejection Emotional Impact

The emotional impacts of church rejection can be profound and multifaceted, affecting individuals' well-being, sense of belonging, and interpersonal relationships. Some of the emotional impacts of church rejection may include:

1. **Feelings of Hurt and Betrayal**: Church rejection can evoke intense feelings of hurt and betrayal, particularly when individuals experience rejection from individuals or communities they trusted and relied upon for support and acceptance.
2. **Loss of Trust**: Experiencing rejection within the church community can erode individuals' trust in their faith community, church leaders, and even in their relationship with God. This loss of trust can lead to feelings of disillusionment and questioning of one's spiritual beliefs and values.
3. **Grief and Loss**: Church rejection can evoke feelings of grief and loss, as individuals mourn the loss of their sense of belonging, connection, and identity within their religious community. This sense of loss can be particularly acute for individuals who have invested significant time, energy, and emotional resources into their involvement in the church.
4. **Isolation and Loneliness**: Rejection within the church community can lead to feelings of isolation and loneliness, as individuals may feel disconnected from their former social support networks and struggle to find acceptance and belonging elsewhere.
5. **Shame and Self-Doubt**: Church rejection can trigger feelings of shame and self-doubt, as individuals internalize the rejection as a reflection of their own inadequacies or unworthiness. This can lead to a negative self-image and diminished self-esteem.
6. **Anger and Resentment**: Individuals may experience feelings of anger and resentment towards those who have rejected them within the church community, as well as towards the church institution itself. This anger can be directed towards specific individuals, church leadership, or the broader religious community.
7. **Anxiety and Stress**: Church rejection can contribute to feelings of anxiety and stress, as individuals grapple with uncertainty about their place within the church community and fear of further rejection or judgment from others.
8. **Emotional Exhaustion**: Dealing with church rejection can be emotionally exhausting, as individuals may constantly struggle to reconcile their feelings of hurt, betrayal, and loss while navigating their ongoing involvement in the church community.

Overall, the emotional impacts of church rejection are complex and deeply personal, affecting individuals' emotional well-being, sense of self-worth, and relationship with their faith community. It is essential for individuals experiencing church rejection to seek support from trusted loved ones, mental health professionals, or spiritual advisors to navigate these emotional challenges and promote healing and resilience.

Church Rejection Emotional Impact Definitions

Let's define each of the emotional consequences of church rejection:

1. **Feelings of Hurt and Betrayal**: Hurt refers to emotional pain caused by rejection or betrayal from trusted individuals or communities. Betrayal involves a breach of trust, leading to feelings of disappointment, disillusionment, and emotional distress.
2. **Loss of Trust**: Loss of trust refers to the erosion of confidence and belief in the reliability, honesty, or integrity of others, including church leaders, fellow congregants, or the religious institution itself. This loss of trust can lead to skepticism, cynicism, and reluctance to engage with the church community.
3. **Grief and Loss**: Grief involves intense emotional suffering and mourning in response to the perceived loss of connection, belonging, or identity within the church community. Loss encompasses the sense of deprivation or separation from something valued or significant, such as relationships, opportunities, or a sense of purpose.
4. **Isolation and Loneliness**: Isolation refers to the state of being separated or disconnected from others, leading to feelings of loneliness, social exclusion, and alienation. Loneliness involves emotional distress and longing for meaningful connections and social support, which may be exacerbated by church rejection.
5. **Shame and Self-Doubt**: Shame is a painful emotion characterized by feelings of inadequacy, unworthiness, or humiliation in response to perceived shortcomings or failures. Self-doubt involves questioning one's abilities, worthiness, or value as a person, often stemming from internalized beliefs about one's perceived inadequacies or flaws.
6. **Anger and Resentment**: Anger is an intense emotional response characterized by feelings of hostility, frustration, or irritation towards perceived injustices, grievances, or offenses. Resentment involves harboring negative feelings and grudges towards those perceived as responsible for causing harm or injury, such as individuals or institutions within the church community.
7. **Anxiety and Stress**: Anxiety involves feelings of worry, apprehension, or fear about future events or uncertain outcomes, leading to physiological arousal and psychological distress. Stress refers to the physical, emotional, and cognitive responses to external pressures or demands, which may be heightened by the anticipation of further rejection or judgment within the church community.
8. **Emotional Exhaustion**: Emotional exhaustion is a state of depletion and fatigue resulting from prolonged exposure to stressors, conflicts, or emotional demands. It involves feelings of being overwhelmed, drained, or depleted emotionally, mentally, and physically, which may result from the ongoing emotional challenges associated with church rejection.

These emotional consequences of church rejection reflect the profound impact that rejection within the church community can have on individuals' emotional well-being, relationships, and sense of self. Recognizing and addressing these emotional challenges is essential for promoting healing, resilience, and well-being among those affected by church rejection.

Church Rejection Emotional Scenarios

The role of a pastor within a church community is one of profound significance, involving spiritual leadership, guidance, and support for congregants. However, pastors themselves are not immune to the emotional impacts of church rejection. When pastors experience rejection within their own congregations, whether through criticism, conflict, or lack of support, the consequences can be deeply felt and far-reaching. In this section, we explore the emotional impacts of church rejection on pastors, examining how rejection can affect their sense of identity, purpose, and well-being. Through analysis and example, we aim to shed light on the unique challenges faced by pastors within their church communities and the importance of providing support, understanding, and empathy for those who shepherd others.

Scenario I: Pastor

Consider Pastor James, who has faithfully served his congregation for many years with dedication and passion. Despite his best efforts to lead, inspire, and support his congregants, Pastor James begins to notice signs of growing discontent and resistance within the church community.

Some members of the congregation express dissatisfaction with his leadership style, criticize his sermons, or challenge his decisions. Others withhold support or participation in church activities, causing Pastor James to feel increasingly isolated and unsupported in his role.

As the rejection from his congregation mounts, Pastor James experiences a range of emotional impacts. He feels hurt and disappointed by the lack of appreciation and affirmation for his efforts. He struggles with feelings of inadequacy and self-doubt, wondering if he is truly fulfilling his calling as a pastor. He grapples with anger and frustration towards those who criticize or reject him, questioning their motives and intentions.

Despite his outward demeanor of strength and resilience, Pastor James carries the emotional weight of church rejection, which takes a toll on his mental and emotional well-being. He finds it increasingly challenging to continue leading with passion and conviction, as the emotional impacts of rejection chip away at his sense of purpose and fulfillment in ministry.

In this example, we see how church rejection can have profound emotional impacts on pastors like Pastor James, who devote themselves to serving their congregations with love and dedication. Pastor James's experience underscores the importance of recognizing and addressing the emotional challenges faced by pastors within their church communities, as well as the need for providing support, empathy, and affirmation for those who lead and shepherd others.

Deacons play a vital role within church communities, often serving as pillars of support, compassion, and service to their fellow congregants. However, even individuals in esteemed positions such as deacons can experience the emotional impacts of church rejection. When deacons face rejection within their own congregations, whether through exclusion, criticism, or lack of appreciation, the effects can be deeply profound and challenging to navigate. In this section, we delve into the emotional impacts of church rejection on deacons, exploring how rejection can affect their sense of identity, purpose, and belonging within the church community. Through analysis and example, we aim to shed light on the unique struggles faced by deacons and the importance of providing support, empathy, and understanding to those who serve in this capacity.

Scenario II: Deacon

Meet Sarah, a dedicated and compassionate deacon who has served her church community faithfully for many years. Sarah has always been passionate about serving others and supporting her fellow congregants in times of need. However, despite her unwavering commitment and tireless efforts, Sarah begins to notice signs of growing distance and resistance within her church community.

Some members of the congregation express skepticism towards her ideas and initiatives, questioning her motives and decisions as a deacon. Others withhold acknowledgment or appreciation for her contributions, causing Sarah to feel increasingly undervalued and misunderstood in her role.

As the rejection from her congregation intensifies, Sarah experiences a range of emotional impacts. She feels hurt and disillusioned by the lack of support and affirmation for her efforts. She struggles with feelings of inadequacy and self-doubt, wondering if she is truly making a meaningful difference in the lives of those she serves. She grapples with frustration and resentment towards those who reject or criticize her, questioning their understanding of her intentions and dedication to her role as a deacon.

Despite her outward appearance of strength and resilience, Sarah carries the emotional weight of church rejection, which takes a toll on her mental and emotional well-being. She finds it increasingly challenging to continue serving with enthusiasm and compassion, as the emotional impacts of rejection chip away at her sense of purpose and fulfillment in ministry.

In this example, we witness how church rejection can deeply affect deacons like Sarah, who dedicate themselves to serving their congregations with love and devotion. Sarah's experience highlights the importance of recognizing and addressing the emotional challenges faced by deacons within their church communities, as well as the need for providing support, empathy, and affirmation for those who serve in this capacity.

Pastors and their spouses often carry significant responsibilities within their church communities, serving as spiritual leaders, mentors, and sources of support for congregants. However, when pastors and their wives face rejection within their own congregations, the emotional impacts can be deeply distressing and challenging to navigate. The rejection experienced by pastors and their wives not only affects their individual well-being but also impacts their marriage, family dynamics, and sense of calling within the church. In this section, we explore the emotional impacts of church rejection on pastors and their wives, examining how rejection can strain their relationship, erode their confidence, and shake their faith. Through analysis and example, we aim to shed light on the unique struggles faced by pastors and their wives and the importance of providing support, empathy, and understanding to those who lead and serve within the church.

Scenario II: Married Couple

John and Emily have been serving as a pastor and pastor's wife, respectively, in their church community for over a decade. They have poured their hearts and souls into ministering to their congregants, offering support, guidance, and love to those in need. However, despite their dedication and efforts, John and Emily begin to notice signs of growing discontent and resistance within their congregation.

Some members of the congregation express dissatisfaction with John's preaching style, criticize Emily's involvement in church activities, or challenge their leadership decisions. Others withhold support or participation in church events, causing John and Emily to feel increasingly isolated and unsupported in their roles.

As the rejection from their congregation mounts, John and Emily experience a range of emotional impacts both individually and within their marriage. They feel hurt and disappointed by the lack of appreciation and affirmation for their efforts. They struggle with feelings of inadequacy and self-doubt, wondering if they are truly fulfilling their calling as pastor and pastor's wife. They grapple with anger and frustration towards those who criticize or reject them, questioning their motives and intentions.

Despite their strong bond and mutual support, John and Emily's marriage feels strained under the weight of church rejection. They find themselves struggling to navigate their individual emotional responses while also supporting each other through the challenges they face. The emotional impacts of rejection threaten to erode their confidence, shake their faith, and strain their relationship with each other and with God.

In this example, we see how church rejection can have profound emotional impacts on pastors and their wives like John and Emily, who devote themselves to serving their congregations with love and dedication. Their experience underscores the importance of recognizing and addressing the emotional challenges faced by pastors and their spouses within their church communities, as well as the need for providing support, empathy, and affirmation for those who lead and serve.

Ushers play a crucial role in welcoming congregants into the church, assisting with seating, and ensuring a smooth flow of events during services. Despite their pivotal role in fostering a welcoming atmosphere, ushers may also experience rejection within their own church community. When ushers face rejection, whether through criticism, exclusion, or lack of appreciation, the emotional toll can be significant. In this section, we explore the emotional impacts of church rejection on ushers, examining how rejection can affect their sense of purpose, belonging, and self-worth. Through analysis and example, we aim to shed light on the unique struggles faced by ushers and the importance of providing support, empathy, and understanding to those who serve in this capacity.

Scenario III: Usher

Meet David, a dedicated usher at his local church who takes great pride in his role of welcoming congregants with a warm smile and helping hand. David has served faithfully as an usher for several years, enjoying the sense of camaraderie and purpose that comes with his role. However, recently, David has begun to notice subtle signs of rejection within his church community.

Some congregants make dismissive remarks about his appearance or question his abilities as an usher. Others seem to avoid interacting with him altogether, preferring to seek assistance from other ushers instead. David starts to feel increasingly isolated and unappreciated in his role, wondering if his efforts to serve are truly valued by his fellow congregants.

As the rejection from his church community grows, David experiences a range of emotional impacts. He feels hurt and disillusioned by the lack of acknowledgment and affirmation for his contributions. He struggles with feelings of inadequacy and self-doubt, wondering if he is truly making a difference as an usher. He grapples with anger and frustration towards those who criticize or reject him, questioning their understanding of his dedication and commitment to his role.

Despite his best efforts to maintain a positive attitude, David finds it increasingly challenging to continue serving as an usher with enthusiasm and joy. The emotional impacts of rejection threaten to erode his sense of purpose, belonging, and self-worth within his church community.

In this example, we see how church rejection can deeply affect ushers like David, who devote themselves to serving their congregations with humility and dedication. David's experience underscores the importance of recognizing and addressing the emotional challenges faced by ushers within their church communities, as well as the need for providing support, empathy, and affirmation for those who serve in this capacity.

Summary

The emotional impact of church rejection extends beyond individuals in leadership positions to include those serving in various roles within the church community, such as ushers. In our exploration of the emotional impacts of church rejection, we have seen how rejection can affect individuals' sense of identity, purpose, and belonging within their religious community. Through the example of David, the dedicated usher, we witnessed the profound toll that rejection can take on individuals who serve with humility and dedication. David's experience highlighted the feelings of hurt, disillusionment, and self-doubt that can arise when one's efforts to serve are met with criticism or indifference.

In understanding the emotional impact of church rejection, it is crucial to recognize the unique struggles faced by individuals serving in different capacities within the church community. Whether pastors, deacons, or ushers, those who serve within the church are not immune to the emotional toll of rejection. Their sense of purpose, belonging, and self-worth can be deeply affected by the rejection they experience from their fellow congregants.

As we conclude our exploration of the emotional impact of church rejection, it is clear that addressing these emotional challenges is essential for fostering a culture of support, empathy, and understanding within religious communities. By recognizing the value of each individual's contributions and providing affirmation and appreciation for their efforts, we can work towards creating inclusive and welcoming church environments where all members feel valued, supported, and respected.

Church Rejection Spiritual Impact

The spiritual consequences of rejection within the church delve into the profound effects that such rejection can have on individuals' faith, spirituality, and relationship with God. In religious communities where acceptance, love, and support are foundational values, experiencing rejection can deeply challenge one's spiritual journey and sense of connection to the divine. In this section, we will explore the spiritual consequences of rejection within the church, examining how it can impact individuals' beliefs, practices, and overall sense of spiritual well-being. Through analysis and reflection, we aim to shed light on the unique struggles faced by individuals grappling with rejection in a spiritual context and the pathways to healing, growth, and reconciliation within the sacred spaces of the church.

Church Rejection Spiritual Impact Definition

Spiritual rejection within the church refers to the experience of feeling excluded, judged, or unwelcome in one's religious community based on one's beliefs, practices, or spiritual experiences. It encompasses instances where individuals feel marginalized, criticized, or invalidated in their spiritual journey within the church context. Spiritual rejection may arise from doctrinal differences, cultural biases, or interpersonal conflicts within the church community, leading to feelings of disconnection, alienation, or doubt regarding one's faith and relationship with God.

Church Rejection Spiritual Impact

The spiritual impact of rejection in the church encompasses a range of effects on individuals' faith, spiritual well-being, and relationship with God. Some of the spiritual impacts of rejection in the church include:

1. **Doubt and Questioning**: Rejection within the church can lead individuals to doubt their beliefs, question their faith, and grapple with uncertainty about their spiritual journey. It may cause individuals to wrestle with existential questions and seek deeper understanding of their beliefs in the face of rejection.
2. **Loss of Trust in Religious Institutions**: Experiencing rejection within the church can erode individuals' trust in religious institutions and leadership. It may lead individuals to question the authenticity and integrity of religious teachings, practices, and communities, leading to feelings of disillusionment and skepticism.
3. **Spiritual Isolation and Loneliness**: Spiritual rejection can contribute to feelings of isolation and loneliness, as individuals may feel disconnected from their faith community and struggle to find support and understanding for their spiritual experiences. It may lead individuals to feel spiritually adrift and longing for a sense of belonging and connection with God and others.
4. **Growth and Transformation**: Despite the challenges of rejection, some individuals may experience spiritual growth and transformation as they navigate their experiences of rejection within the church. It may lead individuals to deepen their spiritual practices, seek new sources of spiritual nourishment, and cultivate resilience and perseverance in their faith journey.
5. **Seeking Alternative Spiritual Communities**: In response to rejection within the church, some individuals may seek out alternative spiritual communities or practices that align more closely with their beliefs and values. It may lead individuals to explore different religious traditions, spiritual practices, or forms of worship in search of greater acceptance and affirmation.
6. **Reconciliation and Healing**: For those who experience rejection within the church, the journey towards reconciliation and healing may involve seeking forgiveness, extending grace, and fostering understanding and empathy within the church community. It may lead individuals to engage in dialogue, reconciliation efforts, and efforts to address systemic issues of exclusion and discrimination within the church.

Overall, the spiritual impact of rejection in the church is complex and multifaceted, affecting individuals' beliefs, practices, and relationship with God. It underscores the importance of fostering inclusive, compassionate, and supportive church communities that embrace diversity, respect individual differences, and cultivate a sense of belonging and acceptance for all members.

Church Rejection Spiritual Impact Definitions

Here's a breakdown of each of the spiritual impacts of rejection in the church:

1. **Doubt and Questioning**: This refers to the uncertainty and skepticism that individuals may experience regarding their beliefs, practices, and the teachings of their faith. Rejection in the church can lead to doubts about the authenticity and validity of one's faith, causing individuals to question fundamental aspects of their spirituality.
2. **Loss of Trust in Religious Institutions**: This involves the erosion of confidence and trust in religious institutions, leaders, and doctrines due to experiences of rejection. Individuals may become disillusioned with the church's teachings and practices, leading to a loss of faith in its ability to provide spiritual guidance and support.
3. **Spiritual Isolation and Loneliness**: This refers to the feelings of separation and disconnection from one's faith community and from God. Rejection in the church can lead to spiritual isolation, where individuals feel alienated and alone in their faith journey, lacking the support and companionship of fellow believers.
4. **Growth and Transformation**: Despite the challenges of rejection, some individuals may experience spiritual growth and transformation as a result. This involves a deepening of one's faith, a renewed commitment to spiritual practices, and a greater sense of resilience and perseverance in the face of adversity.
5. **Seeking Alternative Spiritual Communities**: This involves the exploration of alternative spiritual paths or communities in response to rejection within the church. Individuals may seek out different religious traditions, spiritual practices, or forms of worship that align more closely with their beliefs and values, in search of greater acceptance and affirmation.
6. **Reconciliation and Healing**: This refers to the process of seeking forgiveness, extending grace, and fostering understanding and empathy within the church community. Individuals who have experienced rejection may engage in dialogue and reconciliation efforts to address systemic issues of exclusion and discrimination within the church, leading to healing and restoration of relationships.

Understanding these spiritual impacts of rejection in the church is essential for creating inclusive, compassionate, and supportive church communities that nurture the spiritual well-being of all members.

Church Rejection Spiritual Impact

Let's define and describe each of the spiritual impacts of church rejection:

1. **Doubt and Questioning**: Church rejection can lead individuals to doubt their beliefs and question their faith. They may struggle with uncertainty about the teachings and practices of their religion, leading to a period of introspection and questioning as they seek to reconcile their experiences of rejection with their spiritual convictions.
2. **Loss of Trust in Religious Institutions**: Experiencing rejection within the church can erode individuals' trust in religious institutions and leadership. They may feel betrayed or disillusioned by the perceived lack of support and acceptance from their faith community, leading to a loss of confidence in the church as a source of spiritual guidance and community.
3. **Spiritual Isolation and Loneliness**: Church rejection can create feelings of isolation and loneliness as individuals feel disconnected from their faith community and, in some cases, from their relationship with God. They may struggle to find spiritual companionship and support, leading to a sense of spiritual isolation and a longing for connection and belonging within the church.
4. **Growth and Transformation**: Despite the challenges of rejection, some individuals may experience spiritual growth and transformation as they navigate their experiences within the church. They may deepen their spiritual practices, seek new sources of spiritual nourishment, and cultivate resilience and perseverance in their faith journey, leading to personal growth and spiritual maturity.
5. **Seeking Alternative Spiritual Communities**: In response to rejection within the church, individuals may seek out alternative spiritual communities or practices that better align with their beliefs and values. They may explore different religious traditions, spiritual practices, or forms of worship in search of greater acceptance and affirmation, leading to a journey of spiritual exploration and discovery.
6. **Reconciliation and Healing**: For those who experience rejection within the church, the journey towards reconciliation and healing may involve seeking forgiveness, extending grace, and fostering understanding and empathy within the church community. They may engage in dialogue and reconciliation efforts to address systemic issues of exclusion and discrimination within the church, leading to healing and restoration of relationships and a renewed sense of spiritual wholeness.

These spiritual impacts of church rejection highlight the complex and profound effects that rejection can have on individuals' spiritual well-being and relationship with their faith community. Understanding and addressing these impacts is essential for creating inclusive, compassionate, and supportive church communities where all members feel valued, accepted, and supported in their spiritual journey.

Church Rejection Spiritual Impact Scenarios

Sunday school teachers play a vital role in nurturing the spiritual growth and development of children and young adults within the church community. However, despite their dedication and commitment to serving their students and sharing the teachings of their faith, Sunday school teachers may also experience rejection within their own congregations. The spiritual impacts of church rejection on Sunday school teachers can be profound, affecting their sense of purpose, faith, and connection to their spiritual community. In this section, we will explore these spiritual impacts in greater detail, examining how rejection can challenge Sunday school teachers' beliefs, practices, and overall spiritual well-being. Through analysis and example, we aim to shed light on the unique struggles faced by Sunday school teachers and the importance of providing support, empathy, and understanding to those who serve in this capacity.

Scenario I: Sunday School Teacher

Meet Sarah, a dedicated Sunday school teacher who has been serving in her church's children's ministry for many years. Sarah is passionate about sharing the love of God with her students and helping them grow in their faith. However, despite her best efforts, Sarah begins to notice signs of rejection within her church community.

Some parents express dissatisfaction with her teaching style or curriculum choices, criticizing her approach to Sunday school lessons. Others question her qualifications or judgment, undermining her authority as a teacher and mentor. As a result, Sarah feels increasingly isolated and unsupported in her role, unsure of how to navigate the challenges she faces.

As the rejection from her church community mounts, Sarah experiences a range of spiritual impacts. She begins to doubt her abilities as a teacher and question whether she is truly making a difference in the lives of her students. She struggles with feelings of inadequacy and self-doubt, wondering if she is living up to the expectations of her congregation and fulfilling her calling as a Sunday school teacher.

Despite her deep love for her students and her faith, Sarah finds it increasingly challenging to continue serving with enthusiasm and conviction. The spiritual impacts of rejection threaten to shake her faith and diminish her sense of purpose and belonging within her church community.

In this example, we see how church rejection can have profound spiritual impacts on Sunday school teachers like Sarah, who devote themselves to nurturing the spiritual growth of their students. Sarah's experience underscores the importance of recognizing and addressing the spiritual challenges faced by Sunday school teachers within their church communities, as well as the need for providing support, empathy, and affirmation for those who serve in this capacity.

Church musicians play a pivotal role in enhancing the spiritual atmosphere of worship services, using their talents to uplift congregants and lead them in praise and worship. However, despite their integral role in the church community, church musicians may also experience rejection, which can deeply impact their spiritual well-being and sense of belonging. In this section, we will explore the spiritual impacts of church rejection on church musicians, examining how rejection can affect their faith, creativity, and connection to their spiritual community. Through analysis and example, we aim to shed light on the unique struggles faced by church musicians and the importance of providing support, empathy, and understanding to those who serve in this capacity.

Scenario II: Church Musician

Meet Michael, a talented church musician who has been serving in his church's worship ministry for many years. Michael is passionate about using his musical gifts to glorify God and inspire others through worship. However, despite his dedication and commitment, Michael begins to experience rejection within his church community.

Some congregants express dissatisfaction with his musical style or song selections, criticizing his approach to leading worship. Others question his abilities or suggest that he is not fit for his role as a church musician. As a result, Michael feels increasingly disheartened and discouraged, unsure of how to navigate the challenges he faces.

As the rejection from his church community intensifies, Michael experiences a range of spiritual impacts. He begins to doubt his abilities as a musician and question whether he is truly serving God through his music. He struggles with feelings of inadequacy and self-doubt, wondering if he is living up to the expectations of his congregation and fulfilling his calling as a church musician.

Despite his passion for music and worship, Michael finds it increasingly challenging to continue serving with joy and enthusiasm. The spiritual impacts of rejection threaten to diminish his creativity and passion for music, shaking his faith and connection to his spiritual community.

In this example, we see how church rejection can have profound spiritual impacts on church musicians like Michael, who use their talents to serve and inspire others. Michael's experience underscores the importance of recognizing and addressing the spiritual challenges faced by church musicians within their church communities, as well as the need for providing support, empathy, and affirmation for those who serve in this capacity.

Youth leaders play a significant role in guiding and mentoring young members of the church community, providing support, encouragement, and spiritual guidance as they navigate their faith journey. However, despite their dedication and commitment to serving the youth, these leaders may also experience rejection within their church community, which can deeply impact their spiritual well-being and sense of purpose. In this section, we will explore the spiritual impacts of church rejection on youth leaders, examining how rejection can affect their faith, leadership, and connection to their spiritual community. Through analysis and example, we aim to shed light on the unique struggles faced by youth leaders and the importance of providing support, empathy, and understanding to those who serve in this capacity.

Scenario III: Youth Leader

Meet Emily, a passionate and dedicated youth leader who has been serving in her church's youth ministry for several years. Emily is deeply committed to nurturing the spiritual growth and development of the young members of her congregation, providing a safe and supportive environment for them to explore their faith. However, despite her best efforts, Emily begins to experience rejection within her church community.

Some parents' express dissatisfaction with her leadership style or programming choices, criticizing her approach to youth ministry. Others question her qualifications or judgment, undermining her authority as a youth leader and mentor. As a result, Emily feels increasingly isolated and unsupported in her role, unsure of how to navigate the challenges she faces.

As the rejection from her church community mounts, Emily experiences a range of spiritual impacts. She begins to doubt her abilities as a leader and question whether she is truly making a difference in the lives of the youth she serves. She struggles with feelings of inadequacy and self-doubt, wondering if she is living up to the expectations of her congregation and fulfilling her calling as a youth leader.

Despite her deep love for youth and her faith, Emily finds it increasingly challenging to continue serving with enthusiasm and conviction. The spiritual impacts of rejection threaten to shake her faith and diminish her sense of purpose and belonging within her church community.

In this example, we see how church rejection can have profound spiritual impacts on youth leaders like Emily, who devote themselves to nurturing the spiritual growth of the young members of their congregation. Emily's experience underscores the importance of recognizing and addressing the spiritual challenges faced by youth leaders within their church communities, as well as the need for providing support, empathy, and affirmation for those who serve in this capacity.

SUMMARY

The spiritual impact of church rejection is profound and far-reaching, affecting the faith, sense of purpose, and connection to the spiritual community of those who serve within the church. Through the scenarios of Sunday school teachers, church musicians, and youth leaders, we have seen how rejection can shake individuals' faith, leading to doubt, questioning, and feelings of inadequacy. Despite their dedication and commitment to serving their respective ministries, these individuals have faced criticism, doubt, and rejection from their congregations, which has threatened to diminish their spiritual well-being and sense of belonging within the church community.

However, amidst the challenges of rejection, there is also the opportunity for growth, transformation, and reconciliation. Just as individuals may experience doubt and questioning in the face of rejection, they may also deepen their faith, resilience, and commitment to their spiritual journey. By recognizing and addressing the spiritual impacts of church rejection, we can work towards creating inclusive, compassionate, and supportive church communities where all members feel valued, accepted, and supported in their faith journey.

As we conclude our exploration of the spiritual impact of church rejection, understanding and addressing these impacts are essential for fostering a culture of empathy, understanding, and grace within religious communities. By providing support, empathy, and affirmation to those who have experienced rejection, we can create spaces where individuals feel empowered to continue serving, growing, and thriving in their faith. Through dialogue, reconciliation efforts, and a commitment to inclusivity and love, we can work towards healing the wounds of rejection and building a church community where all are welcome, valued, and embraced.

Rejection Mental Disorders and Illness

Understanding Rejection Mental Disorders

Rejection is a universal human experience that can have profound effects on mental health and well-being. Whether it stems from interpersonal relationships, social dynamics, or institutional structures, experiencing rejection can trigger a range of emotional, cognitive, and behavioral responses that may contribute to the development or exacerbation of mental disorders and illnesses. In this section, we will explore the intersection of rejection and mental health, examining how experiences of rejection can impact individuals' psychological functioning, contribute to the onset or exacerbation of mental disorders, and influence treatment outcomes. Through analysis and example, we aim to shed light on the complex relationship between rejection and mental health and the importance of addressing rejection as a significant factor in understanding and treating mental disorders and illnesses.

What are Mental Disorders?

Mental disorders encompass a broad range of conditions that affect an individual's thoughts, emotions, behaviors, and overall functioning. These disorders can vary in severity and presentation, ranging from mild to severe and impacting various aspects of daily life. Common mental disorders include anxiety disorders, mood disorders such as depression and bipolar disorder, psychotic disorders like schizophrenia, and personality disorders. Each disorder is characterized by specific symptoms and patterns of behavior that may interfere with a person's ability to cope with stress, maintain relationships, work, or engage in other activities. Mental disorders are often diagnosed based on criteria outlined in the Diagnostic and Statistical Manual of Mental Disorders (DSM), and treatment typically involves a combination of therapy, medication, and other interventions tailored to the individual's needs.

Rejection can have far-reaching consequences for mental health, impacting individuals across the lifespan and contributing to the development of various mental illnesses and disorders. For example, repeated experiences of rejection in childhood or adolescence, such as peer rejection or parental neglect, have been linked to the development of anxiety disorders, depression, and low self-esteem later in life. Similarly, rejection experiences in romantic relationships or social settings can trigger symptoms of post-traumatic stress disorder (PTSD), exacerbate symptoms of mood disorders, and increase the risk of suicidal ideation and behavior. The cognitive and emotional responses elicited by rejection, such as feelings of shame, worthlessness, and social isolation, can further fuel the progression of mental illness and interfere with individuals' ability to function effectively in daily life. Thus, understanding the impact of rejection on mental health is crucial for informing prevention efforts, therapeutic interventions, and support systems aimed at promoting resilience and well-being in those affected by rejection-related mental health challenges.

Rejection Related Disorders

Church rejection can manifest in various ways, affecting individuals' sense of belonging, identity, and well-being within their religious community. Recognizing the signs and symptoms of church rejection is essential for understanding its impact on individuals' mental, emotional, and spiritual health. In this section, we will explore the common signs and symptoms of church rejection, ranging from feelings of exclusion and isolation to interpersonal conflicts and spiritual distress. By understanding these indicators, we can better identify and address church rejection within religious communities, fostering environments of empathy, support, and inclusion for all members. Through analysis and example, we aim to shed light on the nuanced manifestations of church rejection and its implications for individuals' overall well-being within the context of their faith community.

- **Anxiety Disorders:**

Church rejection can trigger feelings of anxiety, fear, and apprehension, leading to the development of anxiety disorders such as generalized anxiety disorder (GAD), social anxiety disorder, and panic disorder. Individuals may experience excessive worry about social interactions within their church community, fear of judgment or criticism, or anticipatory anxiety about attending church events or services. These symptoms can significantly impair functioning and quality of life, making it challenging for individuals to engage fully in their faith community.

- **Mood Disorders:**

Experiences of church rejection can contribute to the onset or exacerbation of mood disorders such as depression and bipolar disorder. Feelings of rejection, loneliness, and worthlessness may lead to persistent sadness, loss of interest in activities, changes in appetite or sleep patterns, and suicidal thoughts or behaviors. Additionally, individuals may experience mood swings, irritability, or elevated mood characteristic of bipolar disorder, further complicating their emotional well-being within the church context.

- **Post-Traumatic Stress Disorder (PTSD):**

Traumatic experiences of church rejection, such as spiritual abuse or ostracism from religious community members, can result in the development of PTSD. Individuals may experience intrusive memories, flashbacks, nightmares, and hypervigilance related to their experiences of rejection, leading to significant distress and impairment in daily functioning. PTSD symptoms can interfere with individuals' ability to engage in religious practices or attend church events, further exacerbating feelings of isolation and disconnection.

- **Adjustment Disorders:**

Experiencing church rejection can precipitate adjustment disorders, characterized by emotional and behavioral symptoms in response to stressful life events. Individuals may struggle to cope with the challenges of rejection, leading to feelings of sadness, hopelessness, or anger. They may also experience changes in behavior, such as withdrawal from social activities or conflicts with church members or leaders, as they navigate their experiences of rejection and attempt to adapt to their new circumstances.

- **Substance Use Disorders:**

In some cases, individuals may turn to substance use as a maladaptive coping mechanism in response to experiences of church rejection. Feelings of rejection, shame, or inadequacy may drive individuals to seek solace in alcohol, drugs, or other substances as a means of escaping emotional pain or numbing difficult feelings. Substance use disorders can further compound individuals' mental health challenges, exacerbating symptoms of depression, anxiety, and trauma related to church rejection.

- **Stress:**

Stress is a common human experience that arises from various sources, including work, relationships, and life events. However, stress can also manifest as a rejection disorder, particularly when individuals experience rejection in their social, familial, or religious contexts. In this chapter, we will explore stress as a rejection disorder, examining how rejection-related stress can impact individuals' mental, emotional, and physical well-being. By understanding the unique dynamics of stress as a rejection disorder, we can develop strategies for prevention and intervention to support individuals in managing and mitigating its effects. Through analysis and discussion, we aim to shed light on the complex relationship between rejection and stress and its implications for individuals' overall health and functioning.

Rejection Related Disorders Types and Characteristics

Rejection-related disorders encompass a range of psychological conditions that stem from experiences of rejection, exclusion, or invalidation in social, familial, or religious contexts. These disorders can manifest as acute or chronic stress reactions, mood disturbances, anxiety disorders, or trauma-related conditions, significantly impacting individuals' mental, emotional, and physical well-being. In this section, we will explore the various types of rejection-related disorders and their characteristic features. By understanding the diverse presentations of these disorders, we can better recognize and address the unique challenges faced by individuals affected by rejection in their interpersonal relationships and social environments. Through analysis and discussion, we aim to provide insights into the complexities of rejection-related disorders and their implications for assessment, diagnosis, and treatment.

Disorder Type	Characteristics
Anxiety Disorders	Excessive worry, fear of social interactions, panic attacks, avoidance behaviors, hypervigilance
Mood Disorders	Persistent sadness, loss of interest in activities, changes in appetite or sleep patterns, irritability
Post-Traumatic Stress Disorder (PTSD)	Intrusive memories, flashbacks, nightmares, hypervigilance, emotional numbing
Adjustment Disorders	Emotional and behavioral symptoms in response to stressful life events, difficulty coping, changes in behavior
Substance Use Disorders	Maladaptive coping with rejection-related distress, increased substance use, impaired functioning

This chart provides an overview of the types of rejection-related disorders and their characteristic features. Individuals experiencing rejection may present with symptoms consistent with one or more of these disorder types, depending on the nature and severity of their rejection experiences. Recognizing these characteristic features is essential for accurate assessment, diagnosis, and treatment planning, allowing healthcare professionals to provide targeted interventions and support to individuals affected by rejection-related disorders.

Rejection Related Disorders Scenario

Church rejection can have profound implications for individuals' mental health, contributing to the development or exacerbation of anxiety disorders. For those serving in roles of support and leadership within the church community, such as armourbearers, experiences of rejection can be particularly distressing, leading to feelings of inadequacy, fear of judgment, and apprehension about their ability to fulfill their responsibilities. In this scenario, we will explore how church rejection can manifest as anxiety disorders for an armourbearer, highlighting the unique challenges faced by individuals in this role and the importance of providing support and understanding within religious communities.

Scenario I: Armourbearer

Sarah has been serving as an armourbearer in her church for several years, accompanying the pastor and providing support during services and events. She takes her role seriously, viewing it as a way to serve God and contribute to the ministry of the church. However, in recent months, Sarah has been experiencing increasing levels of anxiety related to her role as an armourbearer.

During a recent church event, Sarah overheard a group of congregants discussing her performance as an armourbearer, criticizing her for being too timid and unsure of herself. Although their comments were not directed at her directly, Sarah couldn't shake the feeling of being judged and found herself replaying their words in her mind repeatedly. She began to doubt her abilities as an armourbearer, questioning whether she was truly capable of fulfilling her responsibilities and meeting the expectations of the church community.

As the weeks went by, Sarah's anxiety continued to escalate. She found herself dreading church events and services, fearing that she would make a mistake or be criticized by others. She began to experience physical symptoms of anxiety, such as racing heart, shortness of breath, and nausea, whenever she was called upon to serve as an armourbearer. Sarah's anxiety began to interfere with her ability to function effectively in her role, causing her to withdraw from church activities and avoid interactions with other church members.

Despite her deep commitment to serving in the church, Sarah felt increasingly overwhelmed and hopeless about her ability to overcome her anxiety. She worried that she would let down her pastor and the church community, further exacerbating her feelings of inadequacy and self-doubt. Sarah realized that she needed support and guidance to address her anxiety and regain confidence in her role as an armourbearer.

Church rejection can have far-reaching consequences for individuals' mental health, including the development of mood disorders. For the children of pastors, who often grow up in the spotlight of their parents' ministry and face high expectations from their congregations, experiences of rejection within the church community can be particularly challenging. In this scenario, we will explore how church rejection can manifest as mood disorders for the children of a pastor, highlighting the unique pressures and vulnerabilities they may face in navigating their mental health within the context of their family's ministry.

Scenario II: Pastor's Children

David and Emily are the children of Pastor Mark and his wife, Sarah, who lead a vibrant and growing church in their community. Growing up in the church, David and Emily have always been deeply involved in their parents' ministry, participating in youth groups, leading worship, and volunteering in various church activities. However, as they entered their teenage years, David and Emily began to experience increasing levels of rejection and criticism from their peers within the church community.

During a youth group meeting, David was teased by his classmates for being the pastor's son, with some questioning his authenticity and sincerity in his faith. Despite his efforts to brush off the comments, David couldn't shake the feeling of being judged and misunderstood by his peers. He began to withdraw from youth group activities and church events, feeling isolated and disconnected from his peers and his faith community.

Meanwhile, Emily struggled with feelings of inadequacy and self-doubt as she compared herself to the other girls in her youth group. She felt pressure to live up to the expectations of being the pastor's daughter, but she never felt like she quite fit in with the other girls. Emily's self-esteem plummeted as she internalized the criticisms and judgments of her peers, leading to feelings of sadness, worthlessness, and hopelessness.

As time went on, both David and Emily began to exhibit symptoms of depression, including changes in appetite and sleep patterns, loss of interest in activities they once enjoyed, and feelings of fatigue and lethargy. Their parents noticed the changes in their behavior and mood, but they struggled to understand the underlying causes of their children's distress. David and Emily felt trapped in a cycle of rejection and despair, unsure of how to break free from the grip of their mood disorders within the context of their family's ministry.

Church rejection can have profound and lasting effects on individuals' mental health, sometimes leading to the development of post-traumatic stress disorder (PTSD). For leaders within the church, such as bishops, experiences of rejection can be particularly traumatic, as they may face intense scrutiny, criticism, and conflict within their congregations. In this scenario, we will explore how church rejection can manifest as PTSD for Bishop Eugene, highlighting the unique challenges and complexities faced by leaders in navigating their mental health within the context of their ministry.

Scenario III: Bishop

Bishop Eugene has dedicated his life to serving his congregation, leading with compassion, integrity, and a deep sense of devotion to his faith. Over the years, he has faced numerous challenges and trials within his church community, from managing conflicts among members to addressing controversial issues within the denomination. However, one particular incident stands out in Bishop Eugene's memory as a turning point in his mental health: the betrayal and rejection he experienced from members of his congregation during a time of crisis.

Several years ago, Bishop Eugene found himself embroiled in a conflict with a group of influential members within his congregation who opposed his leadership and vision for the church. Despite his efforts to address their concerns and seek reconciliation, the conflict escalated, leading to accusations, rumors, and personal attacks against Bishop Eugene and his family. Feeling betrayed and abandoned by those he had trusted and served for many years, Bishop Eugene experienced intense emotional distress and psychological trauma.

In the aftermath of the conflict, Bishop Eugene began to exhibit symptoms of PTSD, including intrusive memories, flashbacks, nightmares, and hypervigilance. He found himself reliving the traumatic events of the conflict, unable to escape the emotional pain and distress they had caused. Bishop Eugene's relationships with his congregation and his faith community became strained as he struggled to trust others and to feel safe and supported in his role as a leader.

Despite seeking therapy and support from trusted friends and colleagues, Bishop Eugene continued to struggle with the lingering effects of church rejection and betrayal. He felt haunted by the trauma of the past, unable to fully move forward in his ministry or find peace within himself. Bishop Eugene realized that he needed to confront the trauma of church rejection head-on and to seek healing and reconciliation in order to reclaim his sense of purpose and integrity as a leader in his faith community.

Church rejection can have significant impacts on individuals' mental health, leading to various psychological disorders, including adjustment disorder. For individuals like Prophetess Rita, who hold positions of spiritual leadership within the church, experiences of rejection or conflict can be particularly challenging, affecting their emotional well-being and ability to fulfill their roles effectively. In this scenario, we will explore how church rejection can manifest as adjustment disorder for Prophetess Rita, highlighting the unique stressors and coping mechanisms faced by individuals in positions of spiritual authority within the church.

Scenario IV: Prophetess

Prophetess Rita has served faithfully in her role as a spiritual leader and counselor within her church for many years, providing guidance, support, and inspiration to members of her congregation. However, in recent months, Prophetess Rita has found herself struggling to cope with mounting stress and emotional turmoil related to conflicts and rejection within her church community.

During a series of prophetic services, Prophetess Rita shared messages of encouragement and spiritual insight with her congregation, only to be met with skepticism and criticism from some members who questioned the validity of her prophecies and teachings. Despite her best efforts to address their concerns and engage in open dialogue, Prophetess Rita found herself feeling increasingly isolated and misunderstood by members of her congregation, leading to feelings of rejection and self-doubt.

As the conflicts within her church community intensified, Prophetess Rita began to experience symptoms of adjustment disorder, including persistent feelings of sadness, hopelessness, and anxiety. She found herself struggling to concentrate and focus during her prayers and spiritual practices, feeling overwhelmed by the emotional weight of the rejection and conflict she was experiencing. Prophetess Rita's sleep patterns became disrupted, and she began to experience physical symptoms such as headaches and stomachaches, further adding to her distress.

Despite her strong faith and dedication to her ministry, Prophetess Rita felt increasingly overwhelmed by the challenges she was facing within her church community. She found it difficult to maintain her usual optimism and enthusiasm for her work, feeling drained and depleted by the constant emotional turmoil and conflict. Prophetess Rita realized that she needed support and guidance to navigate the challenges of church rejection and to regain her sense of peace and purpose in her role as a spiritual leader.

Church rejection can have profound and far-reaching effects on individuals' mental health, sometimes leading to the development of substance use disorders. For individuals in positions of leadership within the church, such as Executive Pastors, experiences of rejection or conflict can be particularly distressing, leading some to turn to substances as a way of coping with emotional pain and stress. In this scenario, we will explore how church rejection can manifest as a substance use disorder for an Executive Pastor, highlighting the complex interplay between rejection, mental health, and substance misuse within the context of ministry.

Scenario V: Executive Pastor

John has served as the Executive Pastor of his church for many years, overseeing the day-to-day operations and providing support to the Senior Pastor and congregation. However, in recent months, John has been struggling with mounting stress and emotional turmoil related to conflicts and rejection within his church community.

During a contentious church business meeting, John found himself at odds with several members of the congregation who opposed his leadership and decision-making. Despite his efforts to address their concerns and seek reconciliation, the conflict escalated, leading to heated arguments and personal attacks against John and his family. Feeling overwhelmed and defeated by the rejection and criticism he was experiencing, John began to turn to alcohol as a way of coping with his emotional pain and stress.

At first, John's drinking was limited to occasional social occasions or stressful events at work. However, as the conflicts within his church community continued to escalate, John found himself relying more and more on alcohol as a way of numbing his feelings and escaping from reality. He began to drink alone at home, using alcohol as a way of self-medicating his anxiety and depression.

As time went on, John's alcohol use began to spiral out of control, leading to significant impairment in his daily functioning and relationships. He began to neglect his responsibilities at work and at home, missing deadlines and appointments and withdrawing from social interactions with friends and family. John's family became increasingly concerned about his drinking, but he dismissed their concerns and insisted that he was fine.

Despite his efforts to control his drinking, John found himself unable to stop, experiencing intense cravings and withdrawal symptoms whenever he tried to cut back. He realized that he had developed a substance use disorder, and that his drinking was only serving to exacerbate the underlying issues of rejection and emotional distress he was experiencing within his church community. John knew that he needed help to address his substance use and to confront the root causes of his addiction, but he felt overwhelmed and unsure of where to turn for support.

Rejection Mindset

A rejection mindset for women refers to a negative belief system or set of attitudes that women may internalize in response to experiencing rejection in various aspects of their lives, such as relationships, career, or personal endeavors. This mindset can manifest in several ways:

1. **Self-doubt:** Women may start doubting their worth, capabilities, or attractiveness, attributing rejection to personal shortcomings or inadequacies.
2. **Fear of failure:** Repeated experiences of rejection can instill a fear of taking risks or pursuing goals, leading to avoidance of new opportunities or challenges.
3. **Comparison with others:** Women may compare themselves unfavorably to others who seem more successful or accepted, exacerbating feelings of inadequacy.
4. **Perfectionism:** Striving for perfection to avoid future rejection can become a coping mechanism, leading to unrealistic expectations and increased stress.
5. **Reluctance to assert oneself:** Fear of rejection may result in hesitancy to assert one's needs, desires, or opinions, leading to passivity or self-silencing in personal or professional settings.

Overcoming a rejection mindset involves challenging these negative beliefs, building resilience, and cultivating self-compassion and self-confidence. It's about reframing rejection as a natural part of life's experiences, learning from setbacks, and embracing one's worth and potential beyond external validation.

Church Rejection Mindset

This chart provides a concise overview of the key components of a rejection mindset for women, highlighting the common negative beliefs and attitudes that may arise in response to rejection experiences.

Rejection Mindset for Women	Description
Self-doubt	Doubting one's worth, capabilities, or attractiveness in response to rejection.
Fear of Failure	Avoiding risks or new opportunities due to a fear of experiencing rejection or failure.
Comparison with Others	Comparing oneself unfavorably to others who seem more successful or accepted.
Perfectionism	Setting unrealistic expectations as a way to avoid future rejection.
Reluctance to Assert Oneself	Hesitancy to assert one's needs, desires, or opinions due to fear of rejection.

Church Rejection Mindset Scenario

Alice recently applied for a promotion at her workplace but was ultimately passed over for the position in favor of a colleague. As a result, she finds herself struggling with a rejection mindset:

1. **Self-doubt:** Alice begins to question her abilities and worth, wondering if she lacks the skills or qualifications necessary for advancement. She starts to believe that she's not good enough compared to her colleague who got the promotion.
2. **Fear of Failure:** Feeling demoralized by this rejection, Alice becomes hesitant to pursue future career opportunities. She worries about experiencing similar disappointments and fears facing rejection again.
3. **Comparison with Others:** Alice constantly compares herself to her colleague who got the promotion, focusing on their strengths and achievements while magnifying her own perceived shortcomings. She feels inadequate and discouraged by the comparison.
4. **Perfectionism:** In an attempt to avoid future rejection, Alice becomes fixated on achieving perfection in her work. She sets impossibly high standards for herself, believing that she must excel in every aspect to prove her worth and avoid being passed over again.
5. **Reluctance to Assert Oneself:** Despite having valuable ideas and contributions to offer, Alice becomes hesitant to speak up in meetings or advocate for herself at work. She fears rejection or criticism and holds back from asserting her opinions or pursuing new opportunities.

In this scenario, Alice's experience of rejection has triggered a rejection mindset characterized by self-doubt, fear of failure, comparison with others, perfectionism, and reluctance to assert herself. Overcoming this mindset will require challenging these negative beliefs and building resilience to pursue future opportunities with confidence and self-assurance.

Church Rejection Mindset Scenario

Sarah has been attending her local church for several years and has been actively involved in various ministries. Recently, she volunteered to lead a new project aimed at serving the community, but her proposal was rejected by the church leadership team. As a result, Sarah finds herself grappling with a rejection mindset within the church context:

1. **Self-doubt:** Sarah begins to doubt her abilities and value to the church community. She questions whether her ideas were not good enough or if she lacks the necessary skills to lead effectively. She starts to feel inadequate and unworthy of contributing to church initiatives.
2. **Fear of Failure:** The rejection of her proposal leaves Sarah feeling discouraged and apprehensive about taking on future leadership roles or volunteering for new projects within the church. She worries about experiencing similar rejections and fears being perceived as incompetent or ineffective.
3. **Comparison with Others:** Sarah compares herself to other church members who have successfully led projects or received approval for their proposals. She perceives herself as falling short in comparison and feels envious of their accomplishments, further fueling her sense of inadequacy.
4. **Perfectionism:** In an effort to avoid future rejection and prove herself worthy, Sarah becomes fixated on striving for perfection in her contributions to the church. She feels pressure to meet unrealistic standards and fears making mistakes or facing criticism from others.
5. **Reluctance to Assert Oneself:** Despite her passion for serving the church community, Sarah becomes hesitant to voice her ideas or take on leadership roles. She worries about facing rejection or disapproval from church leaders and peers and hesitates to assert herself or advocate for her contributions.

In this scenario, Sarah's experience of rejection within the church context has triggered a rejection mindset characterized by self-doubt, fear of failure, comparison with others, perfectionism, and reluctance to assert herself. Overcoming this mindset will require Sarah to challenge these negative beliefs, seek support from trusted mentors or peers, and find ways to continue contributing to the church community with confidence and resilience.

Summary

The exploration of church rejection-related disorders sheds light on the profound impact that rejection, exclusion, and conflict within religious communities can have on individuals' mental, emotional, and spiritual well-being. From anxiety disorders and mood disturbances to post-traumatic stress disorder and substance use disorders, the spectrum of disorders stemming from church rejection is wide-ranging and complex. Individuals serving in leadership roles within the church, such as pastors, prophets, and executive leaders, may be particularly vulnerable to the effects of rejection, facing unique challenges and stressors in navigating their roles and responsibilities.

As we reflect on the scenarios presented and the myriad ways in which church rejection can manifest as psychological distress, it becomes clear that addressing these issues requires a multifaceted approach. It involves creating environments of empathy, understanding, and support within religious communities, where individuals feel valued, accepted, and included regardless of their differences or disagreements. It also necessitates fostering open dialogue, conflict resolution, and reconciliation processes to address underlying issues and promote healing and restoration.

Moving forward, it is crucial for religious leaders, healthcare professionals, and community members alike to prioritize mental health awareness, education, and intervention within religious communities. By recognizing the signs and symptoms of church rejection-related disorders and providing timely support and resources to those affected, we can work towards creating spaces of healing, growth, and belonging for all individuals within the church. Through compassion, empathy, and understanding, we can strive to build communities where rejection is replaced with acceptance, conflict with reconciliation, and despair with hope.

Church Rejection Triggers

Church rejection triggers are events, interactions, or circumstances within the church community that evoke feelings of rejection, exclusion, or invalidation in individuals. These triggers can vary widely in nature and intensity, ranging from interpersonal conflicts and criticism to doctrinal disagreements and social exclusion. Understanding and identifying these triggers is essential for recognizing the sources of church rejection and for developing effective strategies for prevention and intervention. In this section, we will explore the concept of church rejection triggers, examining their impact on individuals' mental, emotional, and spiritual well-being within the context of their faith community. Through analysis and discussion, we aim to provide insights into the diverse array of triggers that can contribute to church rejection and to offer guidance on how to navigate and address these challenges with compassion, empathy, and understanding.

Church Rejection Types of Triggers

Triggers related to church rejection can vary widely in nature and intensity, encompassing a range of interpersonal, doctrinal, and social factors. Here are some common types of triggers related to church rejection:

1. **Interpersonal conflicts:** Arguments, disagreements, or misunderstandings with other members of the church community, including leaders, peers, or congregants.
2. **Criticism and judgment:** Receiving negative feedback, criticism, or judgment from others within the church community regarding one's beliefs, behaviors, or actions.
3. **Doctrinal disagreements:** Conflicts or tensions arising from differences in interpretation of religious teachings, doctrines, or practices within the church.
4. **Social exclusion:** Being left out, marginalized, or overlooked within social circles or church activities, leading to feelings of isolation or rejection.
5. **Discrimination:** Experiencing prejudice, bias, or discrimination based on factors such as race, gender, sexuality, or socioeconomic status within the church community.
6. **Leadership challenges:** Facing challenges or conflicts with church leaders or authority figures, including issues related to decision-making, accountability, or power dynamics.
7. **Betrayal and trust issues:** Feeling betrayed or let down by individuals or groups within the church, leading to difficulties in trusting others and forming meaningful relationships.
8. **Change and transitions:** Navigating changes or transitions within the church community, such as leadership turnover, doctrinal shifts, or restructuring, which may lead to feelings of uncertainty or instability.
9. **Rejection of personal identity:** Experiencing rejection or invalidation of one's personal identity, beliefs, or values within the church community, particularly related to aspects of self-expression or individuality.
10. **Past traumas:** Triggering events or experiences that remind individuals of past traumas or hurts within the church context, leading to re-traumatization or emotional distress.

These triggers can vary in their impact and significance for different individuals, depending on factors such as personal history, cultural background, and individual sensitivities. Recognizing and addressing these triggers is essential for promoting healing, reconciliation, and a sense of belonging within religious communities.

Church Rejection Triggers & Factors

Below is a chart describing triggers related to church rejection and common factors associated with each trigger:

Trigger Type	Common Factors
Interpersonal conflicts	- Differences in opinions or interpretations
	- Miscommunication or misunderstandings
	- Personalities or leadership styles
Criticism and judgment	- Perceived lack of acceptance or understanding
	- High expectations or standards
	- Cultural or generational differences
Doctrinal disagreements	- Interpretation of scripture or religious teachings
	- Theological or doctrinal shifts within the church
	- Traditional vs. progressive perspectives
Social exclusion	- Cliques or social circles
	- Exclusion based on demographics or preferences
	- Limited opportunities for involvement or participation
Discrimination	- Prejudice or bias based on race, gender, or sexuality
	- Unequal treatment or opportunities within the church
	- Lack of diversity or inclusivity policies
Leadership challenges	- Issues with authority or decision-making
	- Power struggles or conflicts of interest
	- Lack of transparency or accountability
Betrayal and trust issues	- Broken promises or confidentiality breaches
	- Disloyalty or disunity within leadership
	- Inconsistencies between actions and words
Change and transitions	- Leadership turnover or restructuring
	- Doctrinal or worship style changes
	- Relocation or merger with other congregations
Rejection of personal identity	- Non-acceptance of individual beliefs or practices
	- Pressure to conform to certain norms or expectations
	- Disapproval of lifestyle choices or personal values
Past traumas	- Previous experiences of rejection or betrayal
	- Emotional scars from past conflicts or traumas
	- Triggers related to unresolved issues or unresolved grief

This chart provides an overview of triggers related to church rejection and common factors associated with each trigger. Understanding these triggers and factors can help individuals and church communities recognize and address the underlying issues contributing to feelings of rejection and exclusion within religious contexts.

Common Church Rejection Triggers

- Criticism or negative feedback
- Being ignored or excluded from social activities
- Feeling dismissed or invalidated in conversations
- Receiving a rejection letter or email (e.g., job application, college admission)
- Being passed over for a promotion or opportunity
- Receiving a breakup or divorce announcement
- Not being invited to events or gatherings
- Receiving a low grade or poor evaluation
- Being stood up or canceled on without explanation
- Feeling misunderstood or misrepresented
- Experiencing betrayal or deception from a trusted individual
- Facing disapproval or disappointment from family members or loved ones
- Being overlooked or disregarded in group settings
- Feeling unappreciated or undervalued in relationships or friendships
- Being rejected romantically or sexually
- Facing discrimination or prejudice based on identity (e.g., race, gender, sexual orientation)
- Receiving harsh criticism or rejection from authority figures (e.g., parents, supervisors)
- Experiencing failure or setbacks in personal or professional goals
- Feeling inadequate or insecure compared to others
- Receiving rejection or judgment from peers or colleagues on social media or online platforms.

These are just a few examples of rejection triggers, and individuals may have their own unique triggers based on their personal experiences, beliefs, and sensitivities. Identifying and understanding these triggers is an important step in managing and coping with rejection effectively.

These rejection triggers in voice and facial expressions can convey negative emotions and attitudes during interactions, leading to feelings of rejection or dismissal. Being aware of these cues can help individuals navigate communication more effectively and foster positive relationships. List of rejection triggers related to speech patterns and body language: If you pay close attention to these triggers, you will identify these signals very clearly.

Speech Patterns:
1. Interrupting or talking over someone
2. Using dismissive language (e.g., "whatever," "I don't care," "it's not important")
3. Ignoring or invalidating someone's contributions or ideas
4. Making sarcastic or belittling remarks
5. Using a condescending tone of voice
6. Criticizing or nitpicking someone's speech or ideas
7. Interrupting eye contact while speaking or listening
8. Avoiding direct communication or giving vague responses
9. Using defensive language or deflecting blame onto others
10. Using negative body language cues while speaking (e.g., crossing arms, avoiding eye contact, leaning away)

Body Language:
1. Avoiding physical contact or proximity
2. Crossing arms or legs in a defensive posture
3. Avoiding eye contact or shifting gaze away during conversation
4. Fidgeting or displaying nervous behaviors (e.g., tapping fingers, bouncing leg)
5. Standing or sitting with closed body language (e.g., turning away, hunching shoulders)
6. Using aggressive body language cues (e.g., invading personal space, pointing finger)
7. Displaying disinterest or boredom through body language (e.g., yawning, checking phone)
8. Exhibiting signs of discomfort or tension (e.g., clenched fists, furrowed brow)
9. Rolling eyes or sighing in frustration
10. Displaying fake smiles or insincere facial expressions.

Church Rejection Triggers Scenario

Church rejection triggers, stemming from a variety of common factors, can profoundly impact individuals within religious communities, leading to feelings of exclusion, hurt, and alienation. These triggers often arise from interpersonal conflicts, doctrinal disagreements, social dynamics, and past traumas, among other factors. Understanding how these common factors contribute to church rejection triggers is essential for promoting empathy, reconciliation, and healing within religious communities. In this section, we will explore a scenario that illustrates how church rejection triggers can manifest through these common factors, highlighting the complex dynamics at play and the potential for growth and understanding amidst adversity.

Scenario I: Parishioner

Emily has been a member of her church for many years, actively involved in various ministries and activities. However, in recent months, she has noticed a shift in her interactions with other members of the congregation, leading to feelings of hurt and rejection. As she reflects on her experiences, Emily realizes that several common factors have contributed to the church rejection triggers she has encountered:

1. Interpersonal conflicts: During a church committee meeting, Emily expressed her opinion on a proposed ministry initiative, only to be met with resistance and criticism from other members. Differences in opinions and communication styles quickly escalated into a heated argument, leaving Emily feeling attacked and misunderstood.
2. Doctrinal disagreements: Emily's beliefs on certain theological matters differ from those of some members of the congregation, leading to tension and conflict within discussions on scripture interpretation and religious practices. Despite her efforts to engage in respectful dialogue, Emily feels marginalized and invalidated for her perspectives.
3. Social exclusion: Emily notices that she is often left out of social gatherings and activities within the church, despite her desire to connect with others and build meaningful relationships. Cliques and social circles within the congregation create barriers to inclusion, leaving Emily feeling isolated and overlooked.
4. Past traumas: Emily's experiences of rejection and betrayal in her previous church community continue to haunt her, triggering feelings of fear and mistrust in her current church environment. Despite her best efforts to move past these traumas, they resurface whenever she encounters situations reminiscent of her past hurts.

As Emily grapples with these church rejection triggers, she realizes the importance of addressing the underlying factors contributing to her feelings of rejection and exclusion. Through open communication, empathy, and a commitment to understanding, Emily hopes to foster healing and reconciliation within her church community, creating a space where all members feel valued, accepted, and included.

Church Rejection In Women and Men

Within religious communities, the experience of church rejection can manifest uniquely for women, influenced by factors such as gender roles, cultural expectations, and theological interpretations. Women within religious contexts often navigate a complex landscape of beliefs, practices, and social dynamics that can contribute to feelings of exclusion, invalidation, or marginalization. In this section, we will explore the phenomenon of church rejection in women, examining the various factors that shape their experiences and the impact it can have on their mental, emotional, and spiritual well-being. Through this exploration, we aim to shed light on the challenges faced by women within religious communities and to provide insights into fostering environments of inclusivity, empowerment, and acceptance within the church.

Within the dynamic tapestry of religious communities, church rejection can wield a profound influence on individuals' lives, shaping their sense of identity, belonging, and spiritual well-being. Women and men within these communities navigate distinct roles, expectations, and challenges, which can influence how they experience and respond to rejection within the church. In this chapter, we will delve into the multifaceted impact of church rejection on women and men, exploring the unique dynamics at play and the implications for their mental, emotional, and spiritual health.

1. **Gendered Expectations and Roles:**
   - Women: In many religious traditions, women may encounter expectations regarding their roles as caregivers, nurturers, and supporters within the church. Church rejection for women may stem from perceived deviations from these roles or challenges to traditional gender norms.
   - Men: Conversely, men may face pressure to embody qualities of leadership, strength, and authority within religious contexts. Church rejection for men may arise from perceived failures to meet these expectations or challenges to their perceived status and authority within the church hierarchy.
2. **Social Dynamics and Power Structures:**
   - Women: Within religious communities, women may experience exclusion or marginalization in decision-making processes, leadership positions, or theological discussions. Church rejection for women may be exacerbated by patriarchal power structures that limit their agency and voice within the church.
   - Men: While men may hold positions of leadership and authority within the church, they may also face pressures to conform to rigid standards of masculinity and emotional stoicism. Church rejection for men may result from feelings of inadequacy or vulnerability that contradict societal expectations of male strength and dominance.
3. **Emotional and Psychological Impact:**
   - Women: Church rejection can have significant emotional and psychological consequences for women, leading to feelings of worthlessness, self-doubt, and internalized shame. Women

may grapple with issues of identity and self-esteem as they navigate the complexities of gendered expectations and societal pressures within religious communities.
- Men: Similarly, church rejection can take a toll on men's mental and emotional well-being, contributing to feelings of isolation, anger, and frustration. Men may struggle to express vulnerability or seek support due to societal stigmas surrounding male emotions and mental health.

4. **Spiritual Consequences:**
    - Women: For women, church rejection may result in a crisis of faith or spiritual disconnection, as they grapple with questions of God's love, acceptance, and inclusion. Women may feel alienated from religious teachings or practices that reinforce patriarchal values or perpetuate gender-based discrimination.
    - Men: Church rejection may also challenge men's spiritual beliefs and convictions, prompting them to reevaluate their relationship with their faith community and their understanding of divine love and grace. Men may seek alternative forms of spiritual expression or community that align more closely with their values and beliefs.

Summary

The impact of church rejection on women and men within religious communities is a complex and multifaceted phenomenon, shaped by intersecting factors of gender, power dynamics, and social expectations. By acknowledging and addressing these unique experiences, religious leaders and communities can strive to create environments of inclusivity, empathy, and acceptance where all members feel valued, respected, and supported in their journey of faith.

Church Rejections Impacts Brain Development

Church rejection can have significant and lasting effects on brain development, influencing neural pathways, cognitive processes, and emotional regulation from childhood through adulthood. Understanding these neurobiological mechanisms is crucial for recognizing the complex interplay between church rejection and brain function and for promoting resilience, healing, and growth within religious communities. In this chapter, we will explore how church rejection impacts brain development across various stages of life, examining the neurobiological underpinnings of rejection-related experiences and their implications for individuals' mental health and well-being.

1. **Neurobiological Responses to Rejection:**
   - Research has shown that experiences of rejection, exclusion, or marginalization within religious communities can activate brain regions associated with emotional distress, such as the anterior cingulate cortex and insula. These neural responses to rejection can trigger physiological stress responses, leading to increased heart rate, blood pressure, and cortisol levels.
2. **Impact on Cognitive Processes:**
   - Church rejection can also influence cognitive processes such as attention, memory, and decision-making. Individuals who have experienced rejection may exhibit hypervigilance to social cues, increased rumination on negative thoughts, and difficulties in focusing attention or regulating emotions. These cognitive biases can perpetuate feelings of insecurity, self-doubt, and worthlessness.
3. **Developmental Consequences:**
   - During critical periods of brain development, such as childhood and adolescence, experiences of rejection can have profound and long-lasting effects on neural connectivity and plasticity. Chronic exposure to rejection-related stressors during these sensitive periods can alter the development of neural circuits involved in social processing, emotion regulation, and self-esteem.
4. **Mental Health Implications:**
   - The neurobiological effects of church rejection can contribute to a range of mental health challenges, including depression, anxiety, and post-traumatic stress disorder. Repeated experiences of rejection can sensitize the brain's stress response system, making individuals more vulnerable to future stressors and increasing their risk for mental health disorders.
5. **Resilience and Healing:**
   - Despite the detrimental effects of church rejection on brain development, individuals also possess inherent resilience and adaptive coping mechanisms that can facilitate healing and recovery. Supportive relationships, positive social interactions, and interventions focused on building emotional regulation skills can buffer against the negative impact of rejection and promote neuroplasticity and growth.

The impact of church rejection on brain development is complex and multifaceted, influenced by a combination of neurobiological, psychological, and social factors. By understanding the neurobiological mechanisms underlying rejection-related experiences, religious leaders, mental health professionals, and community members can work together to create environments of empathy, understanding, and support within religious communities, where individuals feel valued, accepted, and empowered to navigate the challenges of rejection with resilience and grace.

Church Rejection Catastrophizing

These examples illustrate how catastrophizing in church rejection can lead to distorted thinking patterns and exaggerated interpretations of rejection experiences. Recognizing and challenging these cognitive distortions is an important aspect of cognitive-behavioral therapy (CBT) and other therapeutic approaches aimed at addressing rejection sensitivity and related mental health concerns.

Type of Catastrophizing	Description
Personalization	Assuming that rejection or criticism reflects one's inadequacy or worthlessness. For example, believing that not being invited to a social event means that nobody likes you.
Magnification	Exaggerating the significance or impact of rejection. For example, believing that not being chosen for a job interview means that you will never find a job and are destined to fail in your career.
Overgeneralization	Applying a single rejection experience to all future situations, believing that one rejection means inevitable rejection in all aspects of life. For example, believing that being rejected by a romantic partner means you are unlovable and will never find love again.
Catastrophic Future Thinking	Projecting catastrophic outcomes or scenarios based on rejection. For example, believing that being rejected by a friend means you will be lonely for the rest of your life.
Dichotomous Thinking	Viewing situations in extreme black-and-white terms, without considering shades of gray or alternative perspectives. For example, believing that if you're not accepted into a specific college, you are a complete failure.
Emotional Reasoning	Believing that emotions reflect objective reality. For example, feeling rejected by a colleague and concluding that you must be incompetent because you feel bad about it.
Fortune Telling	Predicting negative outcomes without evidence or considering alternative possibilities. For example, assuming that you will be rejected if you ask someone out on a date, without considering the possibility of a positive response.

Church Rejection Strategies

Church Rejection Techniques

Church rejection techniques are strategies or tactics employed within religious communities to exclude, marginalize, or ostracize individuals who deviate from established norms, beliefs, or behaviors. These techniques may be subtle or overt and can have significant psychological, emotional, and spiritual consequences for those targeted. Understanding the dynamics of church rejection techniques is essential for recognizing and addressing harmful practices within religious communities, fostering empathy and support for those affected, and promoting healing and reconciliation. In this section, we will explore the various church rejection techniques, their underlying mechanisms, and the implications for individuals' well-being and spiritual growth within the church.

Church Rejection Common Failures

Church rejection strategies encompass a range of intentional actions or behaviors employed within religious communities to exclude, ostracize, or undermine individuals who deviate from perceived norms or expectations. These strategies can take various forms, from overt acts of exclusion to subtle forms of manipulation and coercion, and can have profound effects on individuals' sense of belonging, identity, and well-being within the church. Understanding the dynamics of church rejection strategies is essential for recognizing and addressing harmful practices, fostering inclusivity and empathy within religious communities, and promoting healing and reconciliation for those impacted. In this chapter, we will explore the different church rejection strategies, their underlying motives, and their impact on individuals and communities within the church.

1. **Exclusionary Practices:**
   - Exclusionary practices are deliberate actions taken to exclude or marginalize individuals from participation in church activities, leadership roles, or social gatherings. These practices may involve explicit bans or restrictions based on factors such as gender, race, sexual orientation, or theological beliefs, effectively denying individuals access to the full benefits of belonging to the church community.
2. **Shunning and Social Isolation:**
   - Shunning and social isolation are strategies used to enforce conformity and discipline within religious communities by ostracizing individuals who question or challenge established norms or authority figures. This may involve withdrawing social support, communication, or fellowship from those deemed disobedient or rebellious, leading to feelings of loneliness, abandonment, and psychological distress.

3. **Gaslighting and Manipulation:**
   - Gaslighting and manipulation tactics involve distorting or denying individuals' perceptions of reality, often to maintain power dynamics or control within the church. This may include undermining individuals' confidence, questioning their sanity, or dismissing their concerns as unfounded or irrational, making it difficult for them to trust their own judgment or seek support from others.
4. **Guilt Tripping and Emotional Coercion:**
   - Guilt tripping and emotional coercion tactics exploit individuals' feelings of guilt, shame, or obligation to manipulate their behavior or decision-making within the church. This may involve using guilt-inducing language, emotional blackmail, or threats of divine punishment to compel compliance or silence dissent, fostering a culture of fear, shame, and compliance.
5. **Weaponizing Doctrine and Theology:**
   - Weaponizing doctrine and theology involves using religious teachings, scriptures, or theological beliefs to justify discriminatory or oppressive practices within the church. This may include misinterpreting or selectively quoting scripture to justify exclusionary policies or discriminatory attitudes towards certain groups or individuals, perpetuating harmful stereotypes and prejudices.

Church rejection strategies are employed within religious communities to enforce conformity, maintain power dynamics, or preserve institutional authority at the expense of individuals' dignity, autonomy, and well-being. By understanding the underlying motives and effects of these strategies, religious leaders and community members can work together to challenge harmful practices, promote inclusivity and empathy, and create environments of healing and reconciliation within the church.

Church Rejection Common Errors

The church is often regarded as a sanctuary of love, acceptance, and belonging, where individuals seek solace, community, and spiritual nourishment. However, despite its noble ideals, the church is not immune to the dynamics of rejection, exclusion, and judgment that plague broader society. In fact, church rejection, whether intentional or unintentional, can have profound and lasting effects on individuals' faith, identity, and well-being, tarnishing the very essence of what the church stands for. In this section, we will explore the complexities of church rejection and identify common errors that churches may make in perpetuating exclusionary practices.

1. **Legalism and Pharisaism:**

    - One common error in church rejection is the tendency towards legalism and Pharisaism, where adherence to religious rules and regulations takes precedence over love, grace, and mercy. Churches may focus more on enforcing doctrinal orthodoxy or moral purity than on extending grace and forgiveness to those who fall short of these standards, leading to feelings of condemnation and alienation among members.

2. **Exclusivity and Cliquishness:**
    - Churches may also fall into the trap of exclusivity and cliquishness, where certain groups or individuals are favored over others based on factors such as socioeconomic status, race, or social connections. This can create an environment of elitism and favoritism within the church, where those on the margins feel unwelcome or undervalued, undermining the church's commitment to hospitality and inclusion.

3. **Hypocrisy and Double Standards:**
    - Hypocrisy and double standards can erode trust and integrity within the church community, leading to feelings of disillusionment and betrayal among members. Churches that preach love and acceptance while practicing judgment and exclusion send mixed messages that can damage individuals' faith and sense of belonging.

4. **Lack of Empathy and Understanding:**
    - Churches may also struggle with a lack of empathy and understanding towards those who are different or struggling, failing to provide the support and compassion needed to navigate life's challenges. This lack of empathy can contribute to feelings of isolation and shame among individuals who are experiencing rejection or hardship, further alienating them from the church community.

5. **Resistance to Change and Growth:**
    - Finally, churches may resist change and growth, clinging to outdated traditions or beliefs that perpetuate exclusionary practices. Failure to adapt to the changing needs and demographics of the congregation can hinder the church's ability to effectively minister to all members and may contribute to feelings of stagnation or irrelevance among younger generations.

Church rejection is a pervasive and complex issue that requires careful attention and reflection from church leaders and members alike. By recognizing and addressing common errors in church rejection, we can strive to create church communities that embody the values of love, grace, and inclusivity that are central to the teachings of Jesus Christ.

Church Rejection Summary

Dealing with rejection is an inevitable part of life, yet it can often feel overwhelming and disheartening. Whether it's a romantic rejection, a professional setback, or a social exclusion, rejection can evoke a range of intense emotions, including sadness, anger, and self-doubt. However, while rejection may feel debilitating in the moment, it also presents an opportunity for growth, resilience, and self-discovery. In this section, we explore a series of practical steps and strategies for effectively coping with rejection and navigating the emotional aftermath with grace and resilience. From acknowledging and validating your emotions to reframing negative thoughts and seeking support from others, each step is designed to empower you to face rejection head-on, learn from the experience, and emerge stronger and more resilient on the other side. Join us as we embark on a journey of self-discovery and personal growth in the face of rejection.

Dealing with Church Rejection

By following these steps, you can navigate rejection with greater resilience, self-awareness, and compassion, ultimately emerging stronger and more resilient on the other side.

1. **Acknowledge Your Emotions:** Allow yourself to feel the full range of emotions that come with rejection, whether it's sadness, anger, or disappointment. Recognize that it's normal to experience these feelings and that they are a natural response to rejection.
2. **Validate Your Experience:** Validate your experience of rejection by acknowledging that it's okay to feel hurt or upset. Avoid minimizing your emotions or dismissing them as insignificant.
3. **Practice Self-Compassion:** Be kind and compassionate toward yourself during this challenging time. Treat yourself with the same kindness and understanding that you would offer to a friend going through a similar situation.
4. **Challenge Negative Thoughts:** Recognize and challenge any negative thoughts or beliefs about yourself that may arise as a result of the rejection. Reframe them into more realistic and positive perspectives.
5. **Focus on What You Can Control:** Shift your focus away from what you can't control, such as others' opinions or actions, and instead focus on what you can control, such as your own reactions and behaviors.
6. **Engage in Self-Care:** Take care of your physical and emotional well-being by engaging in activities that nourish and replenish you. This could include exercise, spending time with loved ones, practicing mindfulness, or pursuing hobbies and interests.
7. **Set Realistic Goals:** Set realistic and achievable goals for yourself to help you regain a sense of control and purpose. Break larger goals down into smaller, manageable steps to make them feel more attainable.
8. **Seek Support:** Reach out to trusted friends, family members, or mental health professionals for support and guidance. Sharing your feelings with others can provide validation, perspective, and comfort during difficult times.
9. **Learn from the Experience:** Reflect on the rejection and look for any lessons or insights that you can glean from the experience. Consider how you can use this experience as an opportunity for growth and personal development.
10. **Keep Moving Forward:** Remember that rejection is not a reflection of your worth or value as a person. Stay resilient and keep moving forward, focusing on your goals and aspirations, and remaining open to new opportunities that may come your way.

Church Rejection Biblical Perspective

Understanding rejection from a biblical perspective offers invaluable insight into the human experience of suffering, resilience, and redemption. Throughout the pages of the Bible, we encounter numerous examples of individuals who faced rejection in various forms, yet found strength and purpose in their faith. In this chapter, we will explore the biblical perspective on rejection, examining key examples from scripture and drawing lessons that resonate with our own struggles and challenges.

Examples of Rejection in the Bible

1. **Jesus' Rejection:** Jesus Christ, the central figure of the Christian faith, experienced profound rejection during his earthly ministry. He was despised and rejected by many, facing opposition from religious leaders, skepticism from his own family, and betrayal by one of his closest disciples. Despite this rejection, Jesus remained steadfast in his mission, demonstrating love, compassion, and forgiveness to all.
2. **Paul's Experiences:** The apostle Paul, one of the most influential figures in early Christianity, also faced significant rejection throughout his life. He endured persecution, imprisonment, and hardship for the sake of spreading the gospel message. Despite facing rejection from both Jewish authorities and Gentile communities, Paul remained unwavering in his commitment to Christ, proclaiming, "For I am convinced that neither death nor life, neither angels nor demons, neither the present nor the future, nor any powers, neither height nor depth, nor anything else in all creation, will be able to separate us from the love of God that is in Christ Jesus our Lord" (Romans 8:38-39, NIV).
3. **Joseph's Story:** The story of Joseph in the Old Testament provides another powerful example of rejection and redemption. Sold into slavery by his jealous brothers and unjustly imprisoned for a crime he did not commit, Joseph endured years of hardship and adversity. Yet, through divine providence and unwavering faith, Joseph ultimately rose to prominence in Egypt, reconciled with his brothers, and played a pivotal role in the fulfillment of God's plan for his people.

By examining these examples of rejection in the Bible, we gain insight into the nature of suffering, the resilience of the human spirit, and the transformative power of faith. As we navigate our own experiences of rejection, may we find hope and encouragement in the stories of those who have gone before us, trusting in God's promise of love, redemption, and restoration.

Understanding Rejection in Church Leadership

Church leadership is a calling that comes with unique challenges, including the experience of rejection from various sources within the congregation and broader community. In this chapter, we will delve into the complex dynamics of rejection in church leadership, exploring its sources, impacts, and implications for the well-being and effectiveness of those called to lead. By gaining a deeper understanding of rejection in this context, we can equip ourselves with the insight and tools needed to support and empower church leaders in their vital ministry.

Sources of Church Rejection

1. **Congregation Members:** Church leaders may face rejection from congregants who hold differing theological beliefs, expectations, or personal grievances. Disagreements over church policies, decisions, or changes in leadership can also contribute to feelings of rejection among parishioners.
2. **Fellow Leaders:** Within the leadership team of a church, conflicts, power struggles, or differing visions for the future may lead to rejection or alienation among colleagues. Competition for authority or influence can create tensions that undermine collaboration and unity among leaders.
3. **Higher Authorities:** Church leaders may experience rejection from higher authorities within their denomination or governing body. Disagreements over doctrinal issues, administrative decisions, or conflicts of interest can strain relationships and lead to feelings of rejection or marginalization.

Impact of Rejection on Church Leaders' Well-being and Effectiveness

1. **Emotional Toll:** Rejection in church leadership can take a significant emotional toll on leaders, leading to feelings of sadness, anger, or inadequacy. The constant pressure to please others or navigate conflict can contribute to stress, burnout, and emotional exhaustion.
2. **Spiritual Strain:** For church leaders, rejection may also provoke doubts or struggles in their faith, causing them to question their calling or the presence of God in their lives. Feelings of spiritual isolation or disconnection can further exacerbate the challenges of leadership.
3. **Impaired Effectiveness:** When church leaders experience rejection, their effectiveness in ministry may be compromised. Emotional distress or distraction can detract from their ability to focus on pastoral care, preaching, or strategic planning, impacting the overall health and vitality of the church community.

By recognizing the sources and impacts of rejection in church leadership, we can begin to address these challenges with compassion, empathy, and a commitment to supporting and empowering those who serve in this vital role. Through open communication, conflict resolution, and a shared commitment to the values of love, grace, and reconciliation, we can create environments where church leaders feel valued, respected, and equipped to fulfill their calling with joy and confidence.

Effects of Rejection on Church Leaders

Church leaders are entrusted with the weighty responsibility of shepherding their congregations, guiding them spiritually, and fostering community. However, alongside the joys and rewards of leadership, they also face the harsh reality of rejection, which can have profound effects on their well-being and effectiveness. In this chapter, we will explore the multifaceted impact of rejection on church leaders, examining its emotional toll, its implications for effective ministry, and its potential to sow conflict and division within the church community. By shedding light on these effects, we can better understand the challenges faced by church leaders and work towards creating supportive and nurturing environments for their leadership.

A. Emotional Toll:

- **Discouragement:** Rejection can erode a church leader's sense of confidence and self-worth, leaving them feeling disheartened and demoralized in their role.
- **Frustration:** Constantly facing resistance or criticism can lead to feelings of frustration and helplessness, as leaders struggle to enact positive change or address concerns within the congregation.
- **Burnout:** The cumulative impact of rejection, stress, and emotional strain can contribute to burnout, leaving church leaders feeling physically, emotionally, and spiritually exhausted.

B. Impediment to Effective Ministry and Leadership:

- **Diminished Focus:** Rejection can distract church leaders from their primary responsibilities, hindering their ability to focus on preaching, pastoral care, and strategic planning.
- **Decreased Effectiveness:** Emotional distress and distraction can impair a leader's effectiveness in ministry, compromising their ability to connect with congregants, inspire growth, and foster community.
- **Loss of Vision:** Rejection may cause leaders to question their calling or lose sight of their vision for the church, leading to stagnation or a sense of aimlessness in their leadership.

C. Potential for Conflict and Division within the Church Community:

- **Strained Relationships:** Rejection can strain relationships between church leaders and congregants, fostering mistrust, resentment, or animosity within the community.
- **Divisive Dynamics:** Conflicts arising from rejection may escalate into larger divisions within the church, pitting members against each other and undermining unity and cohesion.
- **Impact on Ministry Effectiveness:** The presence of conflict and division can detract from the church's ability to fulfill its mission and ministry, hindering its capacity to serve and impact the surrounding community.

By recognizing and understanding these effects of rejection on church leaders, we can take steps to support and encourage them in their ministry, fostering environments of trust, respect, and collaboration within the church community. Through empathy, compassion, and a commitment to reconciliation, we can work towards healing the wounds of rejection and nurturing healthy, vibrant church leadership.

Effects of Rejection on Church Leaders

Category	Effects
Emotional Toll	- Discouragement
	- Frustration
	- Burnout
Impediment to Leadership	- Diminished Focus
and Ministry	- Decreased Effectiveness
	- Loss of Vision
Conflict and Division	- Strained Relationships
within the Church	- Divisive Dynamics
Community	- Impact on Ministry Effectiveness

Biblical Perspective on Rejection for Church Leaders

For church leaders, the journey of leadership is often marked by moments of rejection, opposition, and adversity. However, in the midst of these challenges, they can find solace and guidance in the timeless wisdom of the Bible. In this chapter, we will explore the biblical perspective on rejection for church leaders, drawing inspiration from the experiences of prominent biblical figures who faced rejection in their own ministries. Through their examples and the scriptural guidance they offer, church leaders can find encouragement, perseverance, and renewed strength to navigate the trials of leadership with faith and resilience.

A. Examples of Rejection Experienced by Biblical Leaders:

1. **Moses:** Despite being called by God to lead the Israelites out of Egypt, Moses faced rejection and resistance from both Pharaoh and his own people. His journey was marked by moments of doubt, frustration, and opposition, yet he remained steadfast in his faith and reliance on God's guidance.
2. **Elijah:** The prophet Elijah encountered rejection and persecution from the wicked Queen Jezebel and her supporters. Fleeing for his life into the wilderness, Elijah experienced moments of despair and isolation, yet God sustained him and ultimately used him to proclaim His truth and power.
3. **Paul:** The apostle Paul endured numerous hardships and rejections throughout his ministry, including imprisonment, beatings, and opposition from both Jewish authorities and Gentile communities. Yet, Paul remained undeterred in his mission, persevering through adversity and proclaiming the gospel with boldness and conviction.

B. Scriptural Guidance on Perseverance, Faithfulness, and Reliance on God's Strength:

1. **Perseverance:** "Let us not become weary in doing good, for at the proper time we will reap a harvest if we do not give up" (Galatians 6:9, NIV). The Bible encourages church leaders to persevere in their calling, trusting that God will sustain them and bring about His purposes in His timing.
2. **Faithfulness:** "The Lord is faithful, and he will strengthen you and protect you from the evil one" (2 Thessalonians 3:3, NIV). Church leaders are called to remain faithful to God's calling and His word, knowing that He is their source of strength and protection.
3. **Reliance on God's Strength:** "But he said to me, 'My grace is sufficient for you, for my power is made perfect in weakness.' Therefore I will boast all the more gladly about my weaknesses, so that Christ's power may rest on me" (2 Corinthians 12:9, NIV). When faced with rejection and opposition, church leaders are called to rely on God's strength and grace, trusting that He will work through their weaknesses to accomplish His purposes.

Through these examples and scriptural guidance, church leaders can find encouragement and inspiration to persevere in their ministries, knowing that they are not alone in their struggles and that God's strength is sufficient for every challenge they face.

Biblical Perspective on Rejection for Church Leaders

Biblical Leaders	Examples of Rejection
Moses	- Rejection by Pharaoh and the Israelites
Elijah	- Persecution by Queen Jezebel
Paul	- Imprisonment, beatings, opposition

Scriptural Guidance	Key Verses
Perseverance	"Let us not become weary in doing good, for at the proper time we will reap a harvest if we do not give up" (Galatians 6:9, NIV)
Faithfulness	"The Lord is faithful, and he will strengthen you and protect you from the evil one" (2 Thessalonians 3:3, NIV)
Reliance on God's Strength	"But he said to me, 'My grace is sufficient for you, for my power is made perfect in weakness.' Therefore I will boast all the more gladly about my weaknesses, so that Christ's power may rest on me" (2 Corinthians 12:9, NIV)

Church Rejection Strategies

Rejection is an inevitable part of the human experience, yet it can often evoke intense emotions and challenge our sense of self-worth and resilience. Whether it's a romantic rejection, a professional setback, or a social exclusion, coping with rejection requires emotional resilience, self-awareness, and effective coping strategies. In this section, we will explore a range of coping strategies designed to help you navigate rejection effectively and emerge stronger and more resilient on the other side.

From acknowledging and validating your emotions to challenging negative thoughts and seeking support from others, each coping strategy offers a valuable tool for processing rejection and moving forward with courage and resilience. Whether you're facing rejection in your personal relationships, professional endeavors, or other areas of your life, these strategies can help you navigate the complex emotions and challenges that arise.

Join us as we delve into practical tips, exercises, and examples to help you cultivate resilience, self-compassion, and growth in the face of rejection. By incorporating these coping strategies into your life, you can build the emotional strength and resilience needed to overcome rejection and thrive in all aspects of your life.

Church Rejection Coping Strategies

Coping with church rejection can be a profoundly challenging experience, shaking the very foundation of one's faith, identity, and sense of belonging. Whether facing exclusion, judgment, or ostracism within religious communities, individuals may grapple with feelings of hurt, anger, and disillusionment as they navigate the complexities of rejection. However, amidst the pain and turmoil, there is also opportunity for growth, resilience, and healing. In this section, we will explore strategies and insights for coping with church rejection, drawing upon principles of faith, psychology, and community support to guide individuals through their journey of healing and restoration. By acknowledging the reality of church rejection and offering compassionate guidance for navigating its aftermath, we can empower individuals to find strength, hope, and renewal in the face of adversity within religious communities.

Professionally:
- **Maintain Perspective:** Remember that rejection is a common experience in professional life and does not define your worth or competence.
- **Seek Feedback:** Use rejection as an opportunity to seek constructive feedback and learn from experience. Understand what areas you can improve upon and use it as a growth opportunity.
- **Stay Persistent:** Maintain a positive attitude and perseverance in your professional pursuits. Use rejection as motivation to continue working toward your goals and exploring new opportunities.
- **Network and Support:** Build a strong professional network and seek support from mentors, colleagues, or career coaches who can offer guidance and encouragement during challenging times.

In Relationships:
- **Communicate Openly:** Communicate openly and honestly with your partner about your feelings and concerns surrounding the rejection. Share your perspective and listen to theirs with empathy and understanding.
- **Respect Boundaries:** Respect your partner's boundaries and autonomy, even if it means accepting their decision to reject you. Recognize that everyone has the right to make choices that align with their values and priorities.
- **Focus on Self-Care:** Take care of yourself emotionally and physically by engaging in self-care activities that nourish and replenish you. Practice self-compassion and kindness toward yourself during this challenging time.
- **Seek Support:** Lean on friends, family members, or a therapist for support and guidance as you navigate feelings of rejection in your relationship. Talking to someone who cares about you can provide comfort and perspective.

With Family:
- **Set Boundaries:** Establish healthy boundaries with family members to protect your emotional well-being and maintain a sense of autonomy. Communicate your needs and expectations clearly and assertively.
- **Focus on Healthy Communication:** Engage in open and honest communication with family members about your feelings and experiences surrounding rejection. Validate each other's emotions and perspectives with empathy and understanding.
- **Find Common Ground:** Look for areas of common ground and shared values with family members, even during rejection or conflict. Focus on building connections and fostering mutual respect and understanding.

Internally:
- **Practice Self-Reflection:** Take time to reflect on your thoughts, emotions, and reactions to rejection. Explore any underlying beliefs or patterns that may be contributing to feelings of rejection and work on reframing them into more positive and realistic perspectives.
- **Cultivate Self-Compassion:** Be kind and compassionate toward yourself during times of rejection. Treat yourself with the same warmth and understanding that you would offer to a friend in a similar situation.
- **Focus on Personal Growth:** Use rejection as an opportunity for personal growth and self-improvement. Set goals for yourself and take proactive steps toward achieving them, even in the face of setbacks or rejection.
- **Seek Professional Help if Needed:** If feelings of rejection become overwhelming or interfere with your daily functioning, consider seeking support from a therapist or counselor who can help you explore and address underlying issues in a safe and supportive environment.

By implementing these coping strategies, you can navigate rejection with greater resilience, self-awareness, and compassion, ultimately emerging stronger and more resilient in all areas of your life.

Coping Strategies for Church Leaders Facing Rejection

Navigating rejection as a church leader can be an emotionally challenging experience, testing one's faith, resilience, and sense of purpose. In the face of rejection, it's essential for church leaders to develop coping strategies that help them navigate these difficult moments with grace and resilience. In this chapter, we will explore effective coping strategies for church leaders facing rejection, drawing from both psychological insights and spiritual wisdom. By implementing these strategies, church leaders can find strength, support, and renewed purpose in their ministry despite the challenges they face.

Coping Strategies for Church Leaders Facing Rejection

Strategy	Description
Seeking Support	Church leaders can seek support from trusted mentors, colleagues, or spiritual advisors who can provide guidance, encouragement, and perspective during times of rejection. By sharing their experiences and seeking wise counsel, leaders can gain valuable insights and emotional support to navigate challenging situations more effectively.
Self-Care Practices	Engaging in self-care practices such as prayer, meditation, and exercise can help church leaders manage stress, maintain emotional balance, and cultivate resilience in the face of rejection. By prioritizing their physical, emotional, and spiritual well-being, leaders can replenish their energy reserves and approach challenges with a greater sense of clarity, calmness, and inner strength.
Reframing Perspectives	Church leaders can reframe their perspectives on rejection as opportunities for growth, learning, and personal development. By viewing rejection as a natural part of the leadership journey and focusing on the lessons and insights it can offer, leaders can cultivate a mindset of resilience, adaptability, and humility. This shift in perspective empowers leaders to embrace challenges with courage and optimism, recognizing them as stepping stones to greater maturity and effectiveness in their ministry.
Setting Healthy Boundaries	Setting healthy boundaries and managing expectations is crucial for church leaders facing rejection. By establishing clear boundaries around their time, energy, and emotional resources, leaders can protect themselves from burnout, resentment, and unhealthy patterns of overcommitment. By communicating their needs and limitations assertively and respectfully, leaders can cultivate healthier relationships and create space for authentic connection and collaboration within their ministry context.

By incorporating these coping strategies into their lives and ministries, church leaders can navigate rejection with resilience, grace, and a renewed sense of purpose. Through seeking support, practicing self-care, reframing perspectives, and setting healthy boundaries, leaders can cultivate emotional well-being, strengthen their relationships, and continue to serve with excellence and integrity in their calling.

Church Rejection Coping Strategies Checklist

Navigating rejection can be a daunting and emotionally challenging experience, but having effective coping strategies in place can make a significant difference in how we respond and ultimately overcome these setbacks. In this section, we will explore how to implement the rejection coping strategies checklist to navigate rejection effectively and cultivate resilience in the face of adversity.

Each item on the checklist represents a key coping strategy that can help us acknowledge, validate, and process our emotions, challenge negative thoughts, and take proactive steps toward healing and personal growth. By implementing these strategies into our daily lives, we can build a strong foundation for navigating rejection with grace and resilience.

Throughout this guide, we will delve into practical tips, examples, and exercises to help you incorporate each coping strategy into your routine. Whether you're facing rejection in your personal relationships, professional endeavors, or other areas of your life, this checklist will serve as a valuable resource to support you on your journey toward healing and self-discovery.

Join us as we explore how to implement the rejection coping strategies checklist and empower ourselves to overcome rejection with courage, compassion, and resilience.

Church Rejection Coping Checklist

1. **Acknowledge Your Feelings:**
   - Recognize and accept the emotions you're experiencing as a result of the rejection (e.g., sadness, anger, disappointment).
2. **Validate Your Experience:**
   - Validate your experience of rejection by acknowledging that it's okay to feel hurt or upset.
3. **Practice Self-Compassion:**
   - Be kind and compassionate toward yourself during this challenging time. Treat yourself with the same warmth and understanding that you would offer to a friend.
4. **Challenge Negative Thoughts:**
   - Identify and challenge any negative thoughts or beliefs about yourself that may arise as a result of the rejection. Reframe them into more positive and realistic perspectives.
5. **Focus on What You Can Control:**
   - Shift your focus away from what you can't control (e.g., others' opinions or actions) and instead focus on what you can control (e.g., your own reactions and behaviors).
6. **Engage in Self-Care:**
   - Take care of your physical and emotional well-being by engaging in activities that nourish and replenish you (e.g., exercise, spending time with loved ones, practicing mindfulness).
7. **Seek Support:**
   - Reach out to trusted friends, family members, or mental health professionals for support and guidance as you navigate feelings of rejection.
8. **Learn from the Experience:**
   - Reflect on the rejection and look for any lessons or insights that you can glean from the experience. Consider how you can use this experience as an opportunity for growth and personal development.
9. **Keep Moving Forward:**
   - Remember that rejection is not a reflection of your worth or value as a person. Stay resilient and keep moving forward, focusing on your goals and aspirations, and remaining open to new opportunities.
10. **Celebrate Progress:**
- Celebrate your progress and resilience in coping with rejection, no matter how small. Recognize and acknowledge the steps you're taking toward healing and personal growth.

Church Rejection Coping Strategies for Leaders

Church rejection can be a deeply challenging and disheartening experience for pastors, who are called to shepherd and nurture their congregations with love, grace, and understanding. Whether facing criticism, conflict, or opposition within their congregations, pastors may find themselves grappling with feelings of rejection, doubt, and frustration as they seek to fulfill their ministerial duties. However, amidst the struggles, there are strategies and approaches that pastors can employ to navigate church rejection with resilience, wisdom, and compassion. In this section, we will explore practical insights and suggestions for pastors on how to deal with church rejection effectively, drawing upon principles of pastoral care, leadership, and emotional resilience to guide them through the challenges they may encounter within their congregations.

1. **Cultivate Self-Reflection and Awareness:**
   - Encourage pastors to reflect on their own emotional responses and triggers when facing rejection within their congregations. Developing self-awareness can help pastors better understand their reactions and cope with rejection in a healthy and constructive manner.
2. **Seek Support and Guidance:**
   - Encourage pastors to seek support from trusted mentors, colleagues, or spiritual advisors who can offer guidance, perspective, and encouragement during times of rejection. Having a supportive network can provide pastors with emotional validation and practical strategies for coping with rejection.
3. **Practice Boundaries and Self-Care:**
   - Encourage pastors to set healthy boundaries and prioritize self-care to maintain their emotional and spiritual well-being amidst rejection. This may include taking breaks from ministry responsibilities, engaging in activities that bring joy and relaxation, and seeking professional counseling or therapy if needed.
4. **Foster Open Communication and Dialogue:**
   - Encourage pastors to foster open communication and dialogue within their congregations, creating a safe space for members to express their concerns, questions, and feedback. Transparency and authenticity can help pastors address issues of rejection proactively and foster a culture of trust and mutual respect within the church community.
5. **Lean on Faith and Spiritual Practices:**
   - Encourage pastors to lean on their faith and spiritual practices as sources of strength, comfort, and guidance during times of rejection. Engaging in prayer, meditation, scripture reading, and worship can provide pastors with a sense of perspective and purpose as they navigate the challenges of ministry.
6. **Embrace Vulnerability and Authenticity:**
   - Encourage pastors to embrace vulnerability and authenticity in their leadership, acknowledging their own limitations, mistakes, and struggles with humility and grace. Modeling vulnerability can help pastors foster deeper connections with their congregations and cultivate an atmosphere of empathy and understanding.

Church leadership Rejection Scenario

As church leaders, we often find ourselves confronted with the sobering reality of rejection, whether from congregants, fellow leaders, or external forces beyond our control. In the following scenario, we will explore the journey of Audrea, a dedicated church leader who faces rejection in her ministry. Through Audrea's experience, we will uncover the complexities of rejection in the context of church leadership and the coping strategies she employs to navigate this challenging terrain with faith, resilience, and grace.

Scenario I: Audrea's Journey Through Rejection

Audrea has served faithfully as a youth pastor in her local church for over a decade, pouring her heart and soul into nurturing the spiritual growth and well-being of the young people under her care. With a passion for ministry and a deep love for God, Audrea has dedicated herself wholeheartedly to her calling, embracing the joys and challenges of leadership with unwavering commitment.

However, despite her best efforts and intentions, Audrea finds herself facing unexpected rejection from a segment of the youth group she serves. A group of teenagers, disillusioned and disengaged, begins to voice their dissatisfaction with Audrea's leadership style and ministry approach. Criticisms and complaints about her decisions, teaching methods, and interpersonal skills circulate among the youth, leading to feelings of hurt, frustration, and self-doubt for Audrea.

As the rejection intensifies, Audrea grapples with a whirlwind of emotions, questioning her abilities, her calling, and her worth as a leader. She feels caught in a cycle of disappointment and despair, unsure of how to navigate the turbulent waters of rejection without losing her sense of identity and purpose.

Despite the challenges she faces, Audrea refuses to succumb to despair. Drawing strength from her faith and the support of trusted mentors and colleagues, she embarks on a journey of healing and renewal, seeking God's guidance and wisdom in the midst of adversity. Through prayer, self-reflection, and intentional self-care practices, Audrea begins to find peace and clarity amidst the storm, reaffirming her sense of calling and purpose in ministry.

Ultimately, Audrea emerges from her experience of rejection with a deeper sense of resilience, empathy, and compassion for those she serves. Through her journey, she discovers that rejection, though painful, can also be a catalyst for growth, transformation, and deeper intimacy with God. With renewed faith and determination, Audrea continues to serve faithfully in her ministry, trusting in God's grace to sustain her and guide her every step of the way.

In the tumultuous landscape of church leadership, rejection can pose significant challenges, testing the faith and resilience of even the most dedicated leaders. In this scenario, we will follow Audrea, a seasoned church leader, as she grapples with rejection in her ministry and implements coping strategies to navigate this difficult terrain with grace and strength.

Scenario II: Audrea's Journey Through Rejection and Coping Strategies

Audrea, a devoted church leader with a heart for youth ministry, finds herself facing unexpected rejection from a segment of the youth group she serves. Criticisms and complaints about her leadership style and ministry approach begin to circulate among the youth, leading to feelings of hurt, frustration, and self-doubt for Audrea.

Determined to navigate this challenging situation with grace and resilience, Audrea decides to implement several coping strategies to help her cope with rejection and emerge stronger from the experience.

1. Seeking Support: Recognizing the importance of seeking support during times of difficulty, Audrea reaches out to trusted mentors and colleagues for guidance and encouragement. She shares her struggles openly and vulnerably, allowing others to speak truth into her situation and offer valuable perspective and insight.
2. Engaging in Self-Care Practices: Audrea prioritizes her physical, emotional, and spiritual well-being by engaging in self-care practices such as prayer, meditation, and exercise. She spends time in prayer, seeking God's guidance and strength to sustain her through the challenges she faces. She also makes time for activities that bring her joy and relaxation, helping to alleviate stress and restore balance in her life.
3. Reframing Perspectives: Audrea reframes her perspective on rejection as an opportunity for growth and learning. Instead of dwelling on the negative aspects of the situation, she focuses on the lessons and insights it can offer. She recognizes that rejection, though painful, can ultimately strengthen her character and deepen her reliance on God's grace and provision.
4. Setting Healthy Boundaries: Audrea sets healthy boundaries to protect her emotional well-being and prevent burnout. She communicates her needs and limitations assertively and respectfully, allowing herself space to process her emotions and seek support when needed. She also manages her expectations, recognizing that she cannot please everyone and that rejection is a natural part of leadership.

Through the implementation of these coping strategies, Audrea finds strength, resilience, and renewed purpose in her ministry. Despite the challenges she faces, she emerges from the experience with a deeper sense of faith, empathy, and compassion for those she serves. With God's grace as her anchor, Audrea continues to lead with integrity and courage, trusting in His faithfulness to sustain her through every trial and tribulation.

Summary

Dealing with church rejection can be a daunting task for pastors, but with self-reflection, support, and spiritual resilience, they can navigate the challenges with grace and wisdom. By prioritizing self-care, seeking guidance from trusted mentors, fostering open communication, and leaning on their faith, pastors can navigate church rejection with resilience and compassion, ultimately strengthening their ministries and deepening their relationships within their congregations.

Dealing with Church Rejection

The church deals with rejection in various ways, aiming to address the underlying causes and promote healing and reconciliation within the community:

1. **Pastoral Care and Counseling:**
   - Church leaders provide pastoral care and counseling to individuals who have experienced rejection, offering a safe space to express their feelings, seek guidance, and receive support. Pastors and counselors offer empathy, prayer, and spiritual guidance to help individuals navigate their emotions and find healing.
2. **Community Support and Empathy:**
   - Churches foster a culture of community support and empathy, encouraging members to come alongside those who have experienced rejection with love, compassion, and understanding. Through small groups, prayer groups, and support networks, individuals can find solidarity and encouragement from fellow believers who share their struggles.
3. **Education and Awareness:**
   - Churches engage in education and awareness initiatives to address the root causes of rejection within the community, promoting understanding, empathy, and acceptance of diversity. This may involve hosting workshops, sermons, or discussion groups on topics such as inclusivity, forgiveness, and conflict resolution to foster a culture of grace and reconciliation.
4. **Conflict Resolution and Mediation:**
   - Churches employ conflict resolution and mediation strategies to address conflicts and grievances that may lead to rejection within the community. Trained mediators or pastoral staff facilitate dialogue and reconciliation between parties involved, seeking to resolve differences and restore relationships in a spirit of humility and grace.
5. **Accountability and Leadership:**
   - Church leaders hold themselves and others accountable for their actions and attitudes, striving to create an environment of accountability, transparency, and integrity within the community. By modeling humility, vulnerability, and repentance, leaders demonstrate a commitment to addressing issues of rejection and fostering a culture of grace and reconciliation.
6. **Prayer and Spiritual Warfare:**
   - Churches engage in prayer and spiritual warfare to combat the spiritual forces of division, strife, and rejection that may infiltrate the community. Through corporate prayer, intercession, and spiritual discernment, believers seek God's guidance and intervention in addressing underlying spiritual strongholds and promoting unity and reconciliation within the church.

Overall, the church deals with rejection by prioritizing pastoral care, community support, education, conflict resolution, accountability, prayer, and spiritual warfare, aiming to create an environment of healing, reconciliation, and grace for all members of the community.

Guidelines for Effective Deliverances from Church Rejection

1. **Acknowledge the Reality of Church Rejection:**
   - The first step in effective deliverance from church rejection is acknowledging its existence within the community. Church leaders and members must recognize the prevalence and impact of rejection on individuals' lives and relationships, creating a culture of honesty, openness, and vulnerability where struggles with rejection can be addressed with compassion and grace.
2. **Provide Pastoral Care and Counseling:**
   - Effective deliverance from church rejection involves providing pastoral care and counseling to individuals who have experienced rejection. Pastors, counselors, and trained volunteers offer a safe space for individuals to express their feelings, process their experiences, and receive support, guidance, and prayer for healing and restoration.
3. **Foster a Culture of Empathy and Understanding:**
   - Churches must foster a culture of empathy and understanding, where members are encouraged to listen, empathize, and support one another in times of rejection. Through small groups, prayer circles, and support networks, individuals can find solidarity and encouragement from fellow believers who share their struggles and journey towards healing together.
4. **Address Root Causes and Conflict Resolution:**
   - Effective deliverance from church rejection requires addressing the root causes of rejection within the community and implementing strategies for conflict resolution and reconciliation. Church leaders facilitate dialogue, mediation, and reconciliation between parties involved, seeking to resolve differences and restore relationships in a spirit of humility, forgiveness, and grace.
5. **Promote Education and Awareness:**
   - Churches engage in education and awareness initiatives to promote understanding, empathy, and acceptance of diversity within the community. Workshops, sermons, and discussion groups on topics such as inclusivity, forgiveness, and conflict resolution help raise awareness of the impact of rejection and equip members with tools and resources for fostering healing and reconciliation.
6. **Cultivate a Culture of Grace and Acceptance:**
   - Ultimately, effective deliverance from church rejection requires cultivating a culture of grace, acceptance, and unconditional love within the community. Church leaders and members model humility, vulnerability, and forgiveness, demonstrating a commitment to extending grace and compassion to all who seek refuge within the church's walls.

Summary

Effective deliverance from church rejection is essential for creating environments of healing, reconciliation, and restoration within religious communities. By acknowledging the reality of rejection, providing pastoral care and counseling, fostering empathy and understanding, addressing root causes, promoting education and awareness, and cultivating a culture of grace and acceptance, churches can create spaces where all members feel valued, accepted, and supported in their journey of faith and belonging.

Defeating Church Rejection Scriptures

Defeating church rejection is a vital pursuit for fostering unity, healing, and restoration within religious communities. When individuals experience rejection within the church, whether through exclusion, judgment, or ostracism, it can hinder their spiritual growth and erode the bonds of fellowship that should characterize the body of Christ. However, the scriptures provide powerful insights and principles for overcoming rejection, embracing love, and cultivating a culture of grace and acceptance within the church. In this section, we will explore key scriptures that offer guidance and encouragement for defeating church rejection, empowering believers to walk in love, forgiveness, and reconciliation as they navigate the complexities of community life.

1. **Romans 15:7 (NIV):**
   - "Accept one another, then, just as Christ accepted you, in order to bring praise to God."
   - This verse reminds us of Christ's unconditional acceptance of us and calls us to extend the same acceptance to one another within the church community, regardless of differences or shortcomings.
2. **Ephesians 4:32 (NIV):**
   - "Be kind and compassionate to one another, forgiving each other, just as in Christ God forgave you."
   - This verse emphasizes the importance of kindness, compassion, and forgiveness in overcoming conflicts and relational tensions within the church, pointing to Christ's example of forgiveness as the model to follow.
3. **Colossians 3:13 (NIV):**
   - "Bear with each other and forgive one another if any of you has a grievance against someone. Forgive as the Lord forgave you."
   - Similar to Ephesians 4:32, this verse underscores the need for patience, forbearance, and forgiveness in addressing grievances and conflicts within the church, reflecting the boundless grace and mercy that we have received from God.
4. **Galatians 3:28 (NIV):**
   - "There is neither Jew nor Gentile, neither slave nor free, nor is there male and female, for you are all one in Christ Jesus."
   - This verse highlights the unity and equality that believers share in Christ, transcending social, cultural, and demographic differences, and serves as a powerful reminder of our shared identity as children of God.
5. **1 Peter 4:8 (NIV):**
   - "Above all, love each other deeply, because love covers over a multitude of sins."
   - Love is the antidote to rejection, and this verse encourages believers to love one another deeply, recognizing that love has the power to heal wounds, bridge divides, and restore broken relationships within the church.

Summary

Scripture provides invaluable guidance and encouragement for defeating church rejection and fostering unity, healing, and reconciliation within the body of Christ. By embracing principles of acceptance, forgiveness, unity, and love, believers can overcome rejection and cultivate a culture of grace and acceptance within their churches, reflecting the transformative power of Christ's love in their relationships and community life.

Rejection Self-Help Exercises

Dealing with rejection is an inevitable part of life, and while it can be challenging, there are various self-help exercises and techniques that can empower us to navigate rejection with resilience and grace. In this section, we will explore a range of self-help exercises designed to help identify, process, and overcome feelings of rejection.

From journaling and mindfulness practices to cognitive reframing and self-compassion exercises, each self-help exercise offers a valuable tool for understanding and addressing the complex emotions that arise from rejection. By engaging in these exercises, we can cultivate self-awareness, develop healthy coping mechanisms, and build emotional resilience in the face of adversity.

Join us as we delve into practical tips, examples, and exercises to help you identify and implement effective self-help strategies for coping with rejection. Whether you're dealing with rejection in your personal relationships, professional endeavors, or other areas of your life, these exercises will empower you to navigate rejection with courage, compassion, and resilience. Let's embark on a journey of self-discovery and healing as we explore the power of self-help in overcoming rejection.

Church Rejection Self-Help Exercises

1. **Journaling:** Write about your thoughts, feelings, and experiences related to the rejection. Use prompts such as "How did this rejection make me feel?" or "What lessons can I learn from this experience?"
2. **Mindfulness Meditation:** Practice mindfulness meditation to observe your thoughts and emotions without judgment. Focus on your breath and allow yourself to experience whatever arises without trying to change it.
3. **Positive Affirmations:** Create and repeat positive affirmations to counteract negative self-talk and build self-confidence. Examples include "I am worthy of love and acceptance" or "I am resilient and capable of overcoming rejection."
4. **Gratitude Practice:** Cultivate gratitude by focusing on the things in your life that you're thankful for, even in the face of rejection. Keep a gratitude journal or simply take a few moments each day to reflect on what you appreciate.
5. **Cognitive Reframing:** Challenge negative thoughts about the rejection by reframing them into more positive or realistic perspectives. Ask yourself questions like "Is there another way to look at this situation?" or "What opportunities might this rejection present?"
6. **Self-Compassion Exercises:** Practice self-compassion by treating yourself with kindness and understanding. Imagine what you would say to a friend going through a similar situation and offer yourself the same words of comfort and support.
7. **Visualization:** Visualize yourself overcoming the rejection and achieving your goals and aspirations. Imagine yourself feeling confident, empowered, and successful in the face of adversity.
8. **Physical Exercise:** Engage in physical activity to release pent-up emotions and boost your mood. Choose activities you enjoy, whether it's going for a walk, practicing yoga, or participating in a team sport.
9. **Creative Expression:** Use creative outlets such as writing, art, music, or dance to express your emotions and process the rejection in a constructive way.
10. **Seeking Support:** Reach out to friends, family members, or a therapist for support and guidance as you navigate feelings of rejection. Talking to someone who cares about you can provide validation, perspective, and comfort during difficult times.

These self-help exercises can be customized and adapted to fit your individual preferences and needs. Experiment with different techniques to see what works best for you, and don't hesitate to seek professional help if you're struggling to cope with rejection on your own.

Church Rejection Exercises Implementation

Implementing rejection exercises involves incorporating them into your daily routine and committing to practicing them consistently. Here's how you can effectively implement rejection exercises:

1. **Set Aside Time:** Schedule specific times in your day or week dedicated to practicing rejection exercises. This could be in the morning before starting your day, during a lunch break, or in the evening before bed.
2. **Create a Supportive Environment:** Find a quiet and comfortable space where you can focus without distractions. This could be a designated corner in your home, a favorite coffee shop, or a peaceful outdoor setting.
3. **Start Small:** Begin with one or two rejection exercises that resonate with you the most. Trying to do too much at once can feel overwhelming, so start small and gradually incorporate more exercises as you become comfortable.
4. **Use Reminders:** Set reminders on your phone or write down your rejection exercises in a planner or journal to help you stay consistent. Having visual cues can prompt you to engage in exercises regularly.
5. **Practice Mindfulness:** Approach rejection exercises with an open and non-judgmental attitude. Be fully present in the moment and observe your thoughts, feelings, and sensations without trying to change them.
6. **Stay Consistent:** Consistency is key to reaping the benefits of rejection exercises. Even on days when you don't feel like practicing, try to stick to your routine and trust that the effort will pay off in the long run.
7. **Reflect and Adjust:** After each session, take a few moments to reflect on your experience. Notice any changes in your thoughts or emotions and consider how the exercises are impacting your overall well-being. Adjust your approach as needed to better suit your needs and preferences.
8. **Celebrate Progress:** Celebrate small victories and milestones along the way. Recognize the effort you're putting into your personal growth and acknowledge the positive changes you're experiencing because of practicing rejection exercises.
9. **Seek Support:** Don't hesitate to reach out to friends, family members, or a therapist for support and encouragement as you work through rejection exercises. Having a support system can provide validation, accountability, and motivation to keep going.

By implementing rejection exercises in a consistent and mindful manner, you can develop valuable skills for coping with rejection and cultivate resilience in the face of adversity. Remember to be patient with yourself and trust in the process of personal growth and healing.

SUMMARY

The implementation of rejection exercises is a proactive and intentional approach to coping with rejection effectively. By setting aside dedicated time, creating a supportive environment, and starting small, individuals can gradually incorporate these exercises into their daily routine. Consistency is key, and reminders can help maintain momentum. Practicing mindfulness during exercises allows individuals to observe their thoughts and emotions without judgment, fostering self-awareness and growth. Regular reflection helps track progress and make necessary adjustments, while celebrating small victories encourages continued engagement. Seeking support from friends, family, or professionals can provide validation and encouragement throughout the process. Overall, by implementing rejection exercises with patience, dedication, and mindfulness, individuals can develop valuable coping skills and cultivate resilience in the face of rejection.

Church Rejection Exercises

Implementing rejection exercises involves incorporating them into your daily routine and committing to practicing them consistently. Here's how you can effectively implement rejection exercises:

1. **Set Aside Time:** Schedule specific times in your day or week dedicated to practicing rejection exercises. This could be in the morning before starting your day, during a lunch break, or in the evening before bed.
2. **Create a Supportive Environment:** Find a quiet and comfortable space where you can focus without distractions. This could be a designated corner in your home, a favorite coffee shop, or a peaceful outdoor setting.
3. **Start Small:** Begin with one or two rejection exercises that resonate with you the most. Trying to do too much at once can feel overwhelming, so start small and gradually incorporate more exercises as you become comfortable.
4. **Use Reminders:** Set reminders on your phone or write down your rejection exercises in a planner or journal to help you stay consistent. Having visual cues can prompt you to engage in exercises regularly.
5. **Practice Mindfulness:** Approach rejection exercises with an open and non-judgmental attitude. Be fully present in the moment and observe your thoughts, feelings, and sensations without trying to change them.
6. **Stay Consistent:** Consistency is key to reaping the benefits of rejection exercises. Even on days when you don't feel like practicing, try to stick to your routine and trust that the effort will pay off in the long run.
7. **Reflect and Adjust:** After each session, take a few moments to reflect on your experience. Notice any changes in your thoughts or emotions and consider how the exercises are impacting your overall well-being. Adjust your approach as needed to better suit your needs and preferences.
8. **Celebrate Progress:** Celebrate small victories and milestones along the way. Recognize the effort you're putting into your personal growth and acknowledge the positive changes you're experiencing as a result of practicing rejection exercises.
9. **Seek Support:** Don't hesitate to reach out to friends, family members, or a therapist for support and encouragement as you work through rejection exercises. Having a support system can provide validation, accountability, and motivation to keep going.

By implementing rejection exercises in a consistent and mindful manner, you can develop valuable skills for coping with rejection and cultivate resilience in the face of adversity. Remember to be patient with yourself and trust in the process of personal growth and healing.

Rejection Prevention and Control

Rejection prevention and control strategies aim to proactively address and mitigate the risk of experiencing rejection, as well as effectively manage rejection when it does occur. In the context of the treatment plan for educational consultants, these strategies can help build resilience, enhance coping skills, and promote a healthier approach to professional interactions. Here are some rejection prevention and control strategies:

1. **Establish Clear Communication:** Ensure clear and transparent communication with clients, colleagues, and stakeholders to manage expectations and minimize misunderstandings that could lead to rejection.
2. **Set Realistic Goals:** Encourage setting realistic and achievable goals that align with the consultant's expertise, resources, and constraints. Unrealistic expectations can increase vulnerability to rejection.
3. **Seek Feedback:** Proactively seek feedback from clients, colleagues, and supervisors to identify areas for improvement and address concerns before they escalate into rejection.
4. **Continuous Learning and Development:** Invest in ongoing professional development and skill-building activities to enhance expertise and adaptability in the ever-changing educational landscape.
5. **Build Strong Relationships:** Cultivate strong, positive relationships with clients, colleagues, and stakeholders through effective communication, empathy, and collaboration. Strong relationships can serve as a buffer against rejection and enhance professional support networks.
6. **Maintain Professional Boundaries:** Respect professional boundaries and ethical guidelines to avoid overstepping boundaries or engaging in behaviors that could lead to rejection or conflict.
7. **Adaptability and Flexibility:** Embrace adaptability and flexibility in response to changing circumstances, client needs, and organizational requirements. Being open to new ideas and approaches can help navigate rejection more effectively.
8. **Self-Reflection and Growth Mindset:** Foster a growth mindset by viewing rejection as an opportunity for learning, growth, and improvement. Encourage self-reflection on past experiences of rejection to identify areas for personal and professional development.
9. **Develop Coping Strategies:** Equip consultants with effective coping strategies to manage rejection constructively, such as cognitive restructuring, emotion regulation techniques, and seeking social support.
10. **Monitor and Adjust:** Regularly monitor the effectiveness of rejection prevention and control strategies and adjust as needed based on feedback, outcomes, and changing circumstances.

SUMMARY

By integrating rejection prevention and control strategies into the treatment plan, educational consultants can proactively reduce the likelihood of experiencing rejection, effectively manage rejection when it occurs, and promote overall well-being and professional success.

Church Rejection Management Plan

Managing rejection using the rejection treatment plan involves implementing a comprehensive approach to address the emotional, cognitive, and behavioral aspects of rejection. Here's how to manage rejection using the rejection treatment plan for educational consultants:

1. **Assessment:** Begin by conducting a thorough assessment of the rejection experience, including the circumstances surrounding the rejection, the consultant's emotional response, and any patterns or triggers associated with rejection.
2. **Goal Setting:** Collaboratively set SMART goals with the consultant, focusing on reducing distress related to rejection, improving coping skills, enhancing self-confidence, and fostering resilience in the educational consulting context.
3. **Psychoeducation:** Provide education on the nature of rejection in the educational field, including common triggers, cognitive distortions, and emotional responses. Offer insights into effective coping strategies and resilience-building techniques.
4. **Cognitive Restructuring:** Teach the consultant cognitive restructuring techniques to challenge and reframe negative thoughts and beliefs about rejection. Encourage the development of more adaptive and realistic perspectives.
5. **Emotional Regulation:** Train the consultant in emotion regulation skills such as mindfulness, deep breathing exercises, and progressive muscle relaxation to manage distressing emotions triggered by rejection.
6. **Interpersonal Skills Training:** Provide training in assertiveness and communication skills to help the consultant effectively navigate rejection in professional interactions. Role-playing exercises can be used to practice assertive responses to rejection.
7. **Social Support Enhancement:** Facilitate the identification and utilization of supportive networks, including colleagues, mentors, and professional organizations. Encourage the consultant to seek out social support and share experiences with others in similar roles.
8. **Behavioral Activation:** Assist the consultant in identifying and engaging in pleasurable and meaningful activities outside of work to promote well-being and reduce vulnerability to rejection-related stress.
9. **Relapse Prevention:** Develop a relapse prevention plan outlining warning signs of distress or negative coping patterns associated with rejection. Equip the consultant with coping strategies and resources to effectively manage setbacks.
10. **Follow-Up and Monitoring:** Schedule regular follow-up sessions to review progress, address challenges, and modify the treatment plan as needed. Monitor adherence to treatment strategies and assess overall functioning and satisfaction.

By implementing these components of the rejection treatment plan, educational consultants can effectively manage rejection, develop adaptive coping skills, and foster resilience in the face of adversity. Additionally, ongoing support and collaboration with a therapist or counselor can further enhance the consultant's ability to navigate rejection and promote well-being.

PREVENTIVE SOLUTIONS

Church Rejection Solutions

Preventive care solutions for rejection are essential tools for maintaining emotional well-being and resilience in the face of life's inevitable challenges. While rejection is a natural part of the human experience, proactively addressing its potential impact can empower individuals to navigate setbacks with greater ease and resilience. In this introduction, we'll explore the importance of preventive care strategies for rejection, their role in promoting emotional health, and how they can help individuals cultivate resilience and self-confidence in the face of adversity. From building strong support networks to practicing self-care and fostering a growth mindset, these strategies offer invaluable tools for proactively managing rejection and maintaining overall well-being.

Leaving a Church Effectively after Rejection

Leaving a church after dealing with rejection can be a deeply challenging and emotional process, fraught with feelings of hurt, disappointment, and uncertainty. Whether the rejection stemmed from exclusion, judgment, or conflict within the church community, the decision to leave can be a painful but necessary step towards healing and restoration. In this section, we will explore practical insights and considerations for navigating the process of leaving a church after experiencing rejection, offering guidance and support to individuals as they seek to find closure, peace, and a sense of belonging in their spiritual journey.

Departing a Church Following Rejection:

1. **Seek Closure and Resolution:**
   - Before making the decision to leave, it's important to seek closure and resolution for the rejection you have experienced within the church. This may involve having honest conversations with church leaders or members about your feelings and experiences, seeking apologies or reconciliation where possible, and addressing any unresolved issues or grievances.
2. **Consider Your Emotional Well-being:**
   - Leaving a church can be an emotionally taxing experience, especially after dealing with rejection. Take time to prioritize your emotional well-being and self-care throughout the process. Seek support from trusted friends, family members, or spiritual advisors who can offer guidance, encouragement, and empathy as you navigate this challenging transition.
3. **Reflect on Your Spiritual Needs:**
   - Reflect on your spiritual needs and priorities as you consider leaving the church. What aspects of your faith are most important to you? What kind of spiritual community do you envision being a part of moving forward? Take time to discern what you are looking for in a church and how your decision to leave aligns with your spiritual journey and growth.
4. **Explore Alternative Options:**
   - Explore alternative options for spiritual community and fellowship outside of the church you are leaving. This may involve visiting other churches or religious gatherings in your area, exploring online communities or faith-based organizations, or connecting with small groups or support networks that align with your beliefs and values.
5. **Leave Gracefully and Respectfully:**
   - When the time comes to leave the church, do so gracefully and respectfully, honoring the relationships and experiences you have had within the community. Express gratitude for the ways in which the church has impacted your life and faith journey, and communicate your decision to leave with honesty, kindness, and integrity.

Summary

Leaving a church after dealing with rejection is a deeply personal and sometimes painful decision, but it can also be a necessary step towards finding healing, restoration, and a renewed sense of belonging in your spiritual journey. By seeking closure and resolution, prioritizing your emotional well-being, reflecting on your spiritual needs, exploring alternative options, and leaving gracefully and respectfully, you can navigate this transition with grace, wisdom, and resilience, trusting that God will guide you towards the community where you can truly flourish and grow in your faith.

Leaving a Church Gracefully Following Experience of Rejection

Leaving a church after experiencing rejection can be a difficult and sensitive process, requiring careful consideration and emotional resilience. Whether the rejection stems from interpersonal conflicts, doctrinal differences, or a lack of acceptance within the community, individuals may find themselves grappling with feelings of hurt, disappointment, and uncertainty as they navigate this transition. In this section, we will explore practical insights and considerations for leaving a church after dealing with rejection, offering guidance and support to individuals as they seek to find closure, healing, and a sense of belonging in their spiritual journey.

Leaving a Church After Dealing with Rejection

Consideration	Description
Seek Closure and Resolution	- Engage in honest conversations with church leaders or members about experiences of rejection. Seek apologies or reconciliation where possible. Address unresolved issues or grievances.
Prioritize Emotional Well-being	- Prioritize self-care and emotional well-being throughout the process. Seek support from trusted friends, family, or spiritual advisors. Allow yourself to grieve and process your emotions.
Reflect on Spiritual Needs	- Reflect on your spiritual needs and priorities as you consider leaving the church. Determine what aspects of your faith are most important to you and what type of spiritual community you desire moving forward.
Explore Alternative Options	- Explore alternative options for spiritual community and fellowship outside of the church. Visit other churches or religious gatherings, explore online communities, or connect with small groups aligned with your beliefs.
Leave Gracefully and Respectfully	- Express gratitude for the positive aspects of your time in the church. Communicate your decision to leave with honesty, kindness, and integrity. Avoid burning bridges or causing unnecessary conflict.

Summary

Leaving a church after dealing with rejection is a complex and deeply personal process, but with thoughtful consideration and support, individuals can navigate this transition with grace and resilience. By seeking closure and resolution, prioritizing emotional well-being, reflecting on spiritual needs, exploring alternative options, and leaving gracefully and respectfully, individuals can find healing, closure, and a renewed sense of belonging as they continue their spiritual journey.

Social Media Etiquette When Departing from a Church

Avoiding posting negativity after leaving a church is crucial for maintaining your own emotional well-being and preserving the dignity of all involved. Here are steps to help you navigate this situation gracefully:

1. **Pause Before Posting:** Before posting anything online about your experience leaving the church, take a pause. Avoid posting impulsively in the heat of the moment. Give yourself time to process your emotions and consider the potential consequences of your words.
2. **Reflect on Your Intentions:** Reflect on why you want to share your experience publicly. Are you seeking validation, venting your frustrations, or hoping to initiate change? Consider whether posting online is the most constructive way to achieve your goals.
3. **Focus on Healing:** Instead of dwelling on the negative aspects of your experience, focus on your own healing and growth. Redirect your energy towards activities and practices that promote self-care, self-reflection, and personal development.
4. **Seek Support Offline:** If you feel the need to discuss your experience leaving the church, consider reaching out to trusted friends, family members, or a therapist offline. Having face-to-face conversations with supportive individuals can provide validation and perspective without the risk of public scrutiny.
5. **Practice Empathy:** Recognize that everyone's experience leaving a church is unique, and what may have been hurtful to you may not be the same for others. Practice empathy towards those who may still be part of the church community, as well as those who played a role in your departure.
6. **Choose Your Words Wisely:** If you do decide to share your experience online, choose your words carefully. Avoid using inflammatory language, making personal attacks, or sharing sensitive information that could harm others. Focus on expressing your feelings and experiences in a respectful and constructive manner.
7. **Consider Privacy Settings:** If you feel compelled to share your experience publicly, consider adjusting your privacy settings to limit the audience of your post. This can help prevent unnecessary conflict or drama and give you more control over who sees your content.
8. **Leave Room for Dialogue:** Invite constructive dialogue and feedback from others, but be prepared to engage with differing perspectives respectfully. Avoid engaging in arguments or escalating conflicts online, as this can quickly spiral out of control and damage relationships.
9. **Move Forward Positively:** After sharing your experience, focus on moving forward positively. Resist the urge to dwell on the past or continue rehashing negative experiences. Instead, channel your energy towards building a fulfilling and meaningful life outside of the church.
10. **Practice Gratitude:** Cultivate a mindset of gratitude for the lessons learned and the opportunities for growth that your experience leaving the church has provided. Focus on the positive aspects of your life and the relationships that bring you joy and fulfillment.

Church Rejection Action Plans

Dealing with rejection within a church community can be emotionally challenging and spiritually disheartening. However, developing an action plan to address and overcome church rejection can provide individuals with a structured approach to navigating this difficult experience. In this section, we will explore practical strategies and steps for handling church rejection through the implementation of an action plan. By empowering individuals with tools and resources to confront rejection head-on, we aim to facilitate healing, restoration, and a renewed sense of purpose within the context of their faith journey.

Handling Church Rejection Using an Action Plan

1. **Assess the Situation:**
   - Begin by assessing the nature and extent of the rejection you are experiencing within the church community. Reflect on specific incidents or interactions that have contributed to feelings of rejection, and consider how these experiences have impacted your emotional well-being and spiritual health.
2. **Identify Coping Mechanisms:**
   - Identify healthy coping mechanisms and self-care strategies to manage the emotional stress and distress associated with church rejection. This may include practicing mindfulness, engaging in regular exercise, seeking support from trusted friends or family members, or journaling to process your thoughts and feelings.
3. **Seek Support:**
   - Reach out to supportive individuals within and outside of the church community who can offer empathy, encouragement, and practical assistance as you navigate church rejection. Consider confiding in a trusted pastor, counselor, or spiritual mentor who can provide guidance and support from a faith-based perspective.
4. **Set Boundaries:**
   - Establish clear boundaries to protect your emotional and spiritual well-being in the face of rejection. This may involve limiting your exposure to individuals or situations within the church that contribute to feelings of rejection, and prioritizing relationships and activities that uplift and nourish your soul.
5. **Communicate Effectively:**
   - Practice assertive communication skills to express your thoughts, feelings, and needs with honesty and clarity to relevant parties within the church community. Seek opportunities for dialogue and reconciliation where possible, while also recognizing the importance of setting healthy boundaries to protect yourself from further harm.
6. **Explore Alternatives:**
   - Explore alternative avenues for spiritual growth and community outside of the church community where you experienced rejection. This may involve attending worship services at different churches, participating in faith-based small groups or study circles, or engaging in online communities that align with your beliefs and values.
7. **Foster Forgiveness and Healing:**
   - Cultivate a spirit of forgiveness and compassion towards those who have contributed to feelings of rejection within the church community, recognizing that forgiveness is a powerful tool for healing and liberation. Engage in practices of prayer, meditation, or spiritual reflection to release resentment and bitterness, and to open your heart to the possibility of reconciliation and restoration.

Leadership Skills

Responding to Church Rejection

In the realm of church leadership, navigating rejection is an inevitable part of the journey. How leaders respond to rejection can profoundly impact not only their own well-being but also the health and unity of the entire church community. In this chapter, we will explore effective ways for leaders to respond to rejection with humility, grace, and a commitment to reconciliation and restoration.

Response Strategy	Description
Addressing Conflicts with Humility and Grace	When faced with rejection or criticism, leaders can choose to address conflicts with humility and grace, seeking to understand the concerns of those who reject or criticize them. By approaching conflicts with a spirit of openness, empathy, and humility, leaders can foster dialogue, build trust, and promote unity within the church community.
Seeking Reconciliation and Restoration	Leaders can actively seek reconciliation and restoration within the church community, working to mend broken relationships and heal wounds caused by rejection. By extending grace, forgiveness, and understanding to those who reject or criticize them, leaders can demonstrate Christlike love and humility, fostering a culture of reconciliation and unity within the church.
Leading by Example in Demonstrating Forgiveness and Love	Leaders can lead by example in demonstrating forgiveness and love toward those who reject or criticize them. By modeling Christlike character and behavior, leaders can inspire others to respond to rejection with grace, compassion, and a commitment to reconciliation. Through their actions and attitudes, leaders can create a culture of love, forgiveness, and unity within the church community.

By implementing these response strategies, church leaders can navigate rejection with grace, humility, and a commitment to reconciliation and restoration. By addressing conflicts with humility and grace, seeking reconciliation and restoration, and leading by example in demonstrating forgiveness and love, leaders can promote unity, healing, and spiritual growth within the church community.

Building Resilience in Church Leadership

Church leadership is a calling that comes with its share of challenges, including rejection, criticism, and adversity. Building resilience is essential for leaders to navigate these challenges with strength, perseverance, and grace. In this chapter, we will explore strategies for building resilience in church leadership, equipping leaders to thrive in the face of adversity and uncertainty.

A. **Developing a Strong Support Network:** One key aspect of building resilience is developing a strong support network within the church and beyond. Leaders can cultivate relationships with fellow leaders, mentors, and trusted advisors who can offer encouragement, wisdom, and perspective during times of difficulty. By surrounding themselves with a supportive community, leaders can find strength and solace in times of adversity.

B. **Investing in Ongoing Personal and Professional Development:** Another important strategy for building resilience is investing in ongoing personal and professional development. Leaders can pursue opportunities for learning, growth, and skill development that enhance their effectiveness and resilience in ministry. Whether through attending conferences, participating in training programs, or seeking out mentorship, leaders can continuously strengthen their capacity to navigate challenges with wisdom and confidence.

C. **Cultivating a Deep Sense of Purpose and Calling in Ministry:** Finally, building resilience in church leadership involves cultivating a deep sense of purpose and calling in ministry. Leaders can draw strength and resilience from a clear understanding of their mission and vision, grounded in their faith and commitment to serving God and others. By staying connected to their sense of calling, leaders can persevere through challenges with courage, conviction, and hope.

By implementing these strategies for building resilience, church leaders can navigate the ups and downs of leadership with grace, perseverance, and effectiveness. Through developing a strong support network, investing in personal and professional development, and cultivating a deep sense of purpose and calling in ministry, leaders can build the resilience they need to thrive in their roles and make a lasting impact in the lives of those they serve.

Summary

In the face of rejection, church leaders can employ several effective coping strategies to navigate the challenges with resilience and grace. Seeking support from trusted mentors, colleagues, or spiritual advisors provides leaders with guidance, encouragement, and valuable perspective. Engaging in self-care practices, such as prayer, meditation, and exercise, helps leaders manage stress and maintain emotional balance. Reframing perspectives on rejection as opportunities for growth and learning allows leaders to find meaning and purpose in difficult situations. Setting healthy boundaries and managing expectations protects leaders from burnout and fosters healthier relationships within the church community. By implementing these coping strategies, church leaders can navigate rejection with strength, resilience, and a renewed sense of purpose in their ministry.

Navigating Church Rejection: Do's and Don't

Navigating church rejection can be a challenging and sensitive process, requiring wisdom, discernment, and grace. While it's natural to feel hurt, disappointed, or even angry in the face of rejection within a church community, how we choose to respond can significantly impact our emotional well-being, spiritual growth, and relationships within the church. In this section, we will explore a practical guide of church rejection do's and don'ts, offering insights and principles for handling rejection in a manner that promotes healing, reconciliation, and restoration within the context of our faith.

Do's:

1. **Do Seek Support:**
    - Reach out to trusted friends, family members, or spiritual mentors who can offer empathy, encouragement, and practical support as you navigate church rejection. Surround yourself with individuals who will uplift and support you during this challenging time.
2. **Do Practice Self-Care:**
    - Prioritize your emotional and spiritual well-being by engaging in activities that promote self-care and stress relief. Whether it's through prayer, meditation, exercise, or spending time in nature, make time for activities that nourish and replenish your soul.
3. **Do Seek Understanding:**
    - Seek to understand the root causes of rejection within the church community, whether they stem from interpersonal conflicts, doctrinal differences, or cultural biases. Approach the situation with humility, openness, and a willingness to listen to others' perspectives.
4. **Do Set Boundaries:**
    - Establish clear boundaries to protect your emotional and spiritual well-being in the face of rejection. This may involve limiting your exposure to individuals or situations within the church that contribute to feelings of rejection, and prioritizing relationships and activities that uplift and nourish your soul.
5. **Do Foster Forgiveness:**
    - Cultivate a spirit of forgiveness towards those who have contributed to feelings of rejection within the church community, recognizing that forgiveness is a powerful tool for healing and liberation. Release resentment and bitterness, and open your heart to the possibility of reconciliation and restoration.

Don't:

1. **Don't Retaliate or Seek Revenge:**
   - Resist the temptation to retaliate or seek revenge against those who have rejected or hurt you within the church community. Instead, choose to respond with grace, humility, and a spirit of forgiveness, trusting that God will bring about justice and reconciliation in His timing.
2. **Don't Isolate Yourself:**
   - Avoid isolating yourself or withdrawing from community life in response to rejection. Instead, seek out opportunities for fellowship, connection, and service within the church community, and allow yourself to be supported and uplifted by others who share your faith journey.
3. **Don't Suppress Your Feelings:**
   - Don't suppress or ignore your feelings of hurt, anger, or disappointment in response to rejection. Instead, allow yourself to acknowledge and process these emotions in healthy and constructive ways, whether through prayer, journaling, or seeking support from trusted friends or counselors.
4. **Don't Engage in Gossip or Slander**:
   - Refrain from engaging in gossip, slander, or negative talk about those who have rejected or hurt you within the church community. Instead, choose to speak words of kindness, grace, and encouragement, and seek to build up rather than tear down others with your words.
5. **Don't Lose Sight of God's Love:**
   - Above all, don't lose sight of God's love and grace towards you, even in the midst of rejection. Remember that you are deeply loved and valued by God, and that His acceptance is the ultimate source of your identity and worth. Draw near to Him in prayer, worship, and reflection, and allow His love to sustain and empower you as you navigate church rejection with faith and resilience.

Summary

By adhering to these church rejection do's and don'ts, individuals can navigate rejection within the church community with wisdom, grace, and integrity, promoting healing, reconciliation, and restoration within themselves and their relationships. By seeking support, practicing self-care, seeking understanding, setting boundaries, fostering forgiveness, avoiding retaliation or isolation, refraining from gossip or slander, and remaining anchored in God's love and grace, individuals can navigate church rejection in a manner that honors God and promotes peace and unity within the body of Christ.

Church Rejection Signs

Navigating the complexities of church rejection can be a deeply challenging and emotionally tumultuous experience. Whether it stems from conflicts with church leadership, disagreements over doctrine, or feeling marginalized within the congregation, the pain of rejection within a religious community can have profound effects on one's well-being and sense of identity.

In this chapter, we will explore the signs and indicators that may suggest you are dealing with church rejection. By identifying these signs early on, you can begin to address and navigate the emotions, challenges, and complexities associated with rejection in a constructive and proactive manner.

Through self-awareness, introspection, and a willingness to confront difficult truths, you can gain clarity on your experiences and take steps towards healing, growth, and empowerment. Remember, you are not alone in your journey, and there is hope and support available to guide you through this difficult time.

1. **Feelings of Isolation:** You may feel isolated or excluded from the church community, experiencing a sense of disconnect or alienation from those around you.
2. **Emotional Distress:** Dealing with church rejection can evoke intense emotions such as sadness, anger, or despair, impacting your overall emotional well-being.
3. **Decreased Participation:** You may find yourself withdrawing from church activities, services, or events, feeling reluctant or hesitant to engage with the community.
4. **Spiritual Doubt:** Experiencing rejection within the church can lead to doubts about your faith, spirituality, or beliefs, causing you to question your place within the religious community.
5. **Strained Relationships:** Church rejection can strain relationships with fellow church members or leaders, leading to conflict, tension, or breakdowns in communication.
6. **Loss of Identity:** You may struggle with a sense of identity crisis, feeling uncertain about your role or purpose within the church and questioning your sense of belonging.
7. **Physical Symptoms:** Dealing with church rejection can manifest in physical symptoms such as headaches, fatigue, or gastrointestinal issues, reflecting the toll that emotional distress can take on your body.

Recognizing these signs can help you acknowledge and address the impact of church rejection on your life and well-being. Seeking support from trusted friends, family members, or a therapist can provide validation, guidance, and healing as you navigate through this challenging experience.

Church Rejection
Critical Conversations

Critical conversations about church rejection are often necessary but can be daunting. When facing rejection within a church community, individuals may feel hesitant or unsure about how to broach the topic with others involved. However, these conversations are essential for fostering understanding, reconciliation, and healing within the community. In this chapter, we will explore practical strategies and guidelines for engaging in critical conversations about church rejection. From setting the stage to active listening techniques, these insights will equip individuals with the tools they need to navigate these sensitive conversations with courage, compassion, and grace.

Navigating Critical Conversations About Church Rejection

1. **Setting the Stage:**
   - Begin by creating a safe and conducive environment for the conversation. Choose a private and neutral setting where all parties involved can speak openly and honestly without fear of judgment or interruption.
2. **Clarifying Intentions:**
   - Clarify the purpose and intentions behind the conversation. Are you seeking understanding, reconciliation, or resolution? Communicate your intentions clearly and respectfully to all parties involved to ensure alignment and mutual respect.
3. **Active Listening:**
   - Practice active listening skills to ensure that all voices are heard and understood. Listen empathetically, without interrupting or formulating responses in your mind. Reflect back what you've heard to confirm understanding and demonstrate empathy.
4. **Expressing Feelings:**
   - Share your thoughts, feelings, and experiences in a respectful and non-confrontational manner. Use "I" statements to express your perspective without assigning blame or judgment to others. Focus on expressing your emotions and experiences rather than attacking or accusing others.
5. **Seeking Understanding:**
   - Seek to understand the perspectives and experiences of others involved in the rejection. Ask open-ended questions and listen attentively to their responses. Avoid making assumptions or jumping to conclusions, and approach the conversation with genuine curiosity and empathy.
6. **Finding Common Ground:**
   - Look for areas of common ground and shared values that can serve as a foundation for reconciliation and healing. Focus on areas where you can agree or find mutual understanding, and explore possibilities for moving forward together in a positive and constructive manner.
7. **Setting Boundaries:**
   - Establish clear boundaries for the conversation to ensure that it remains respectful and productive. Address any behaviors or language that veers into disrespect or hostility, and reaffirm the importance of maintaining a safe and respectful dialogue.

8. **Committing to Action:**
   - Identify actionable steps and commitments that all parties can take to address the issues raised in the conversation. Agree on concrete measures for reconciliation, resolution, or healing, and establish timelines and accountability measures to ensure follow-through.

Summary

By following these guidelines for navigating critical conversations about church rejection, individuals can foster understanding, reconciliation, and healing within the community. By setting the stage, clarifying intentions, practicing active listening, expressing feelings, seeking understanding, finding common ground, setting boundaries, and committing to action, individuals can engage in these sensitive conversations with courage, compassion, and grace, paving the way for greater unity and wholeness within the church community. In conclusion, navigating the complexities of church rejection is a journey marked by emotional challenges, spiritual growth, and personal resilience. Throughout this book, we've explored the myriad of experiences and emotions associated with leaving a church, from hurt and anger to healing and hope. We've discussed practical strategies for managing emotions, seeking support, and finding meaning during adversity. Remember, your experience of church rejection does not define you, but rather serves as a catalyst for personal growth and transformation. As you continue your path forward, may you find strength, courage, and grace to embrace new opportunities, forge meaningful connections, and discover the abundant blessings that await you on the journey ahead.

Rejection Tips & Techniques

Bonus Edition

Rejection Tip & Techniques

In the intricate landscape of church rejection, individuals often find themselves grappling with a myriad of emotions, uncertainties, and challenges. As they navigate this delicate terrain, practical tips and techniques can serve as valuable guiding lights, offering clarity, resilience, and empowerment. In this chapter section, aptly titled "Rejection Tips and Techniques," we will delve into actionable strategies and insights designed to help individuals effectively navigate and overcome rejection within the church community. From communication tactics to self-care practices, these tips and techniques aim to empower individuals to navigate rejection with grace, courage, and resilience.

Rejection in the Workplace

Promoting mental health in the workplace and fostering employee well-being involves implementing strategies to support individuals in dealing with rejection effectively. Here are some strategies specifically tailored to address rejection in the workplace:

1. **Create a Supportive Environment:** Foster a culture of inclusivity, empathy, and support where employees feel comfortable expressing their emotions and discussing challenges, including experiences of rejection.
2. **Provide Training and Education:** Offer workshops, seminars, or training sessions to educate employees about coping with rejection, building resilience, and maintaining mental well-being. Equip them with practical strategies and resources to navigate rejection in the workplace.
3. **Encourage Open Communication:** Promote open and transparent communication channels where employees can discuss concerns, seek feedback, and express emotions related to rejection. Encourage managers to provide constructive feedback and support to employees facing rejection.
4. **Implement Stress Management Programs:** Offer stress management programs or resources such as mindfulness meditation sessions, yoga classes, or relaxation techniques to help employees cope with rejection-related stress and anxiety.
5. **Offer Employee Assistance Programs (EAPs):** Provide access to confidential counseling services and mental health resources through EAPs. Ensure that employees are aware of these services and feel comfortable seeking support when needed.
6. **Promote Work-Life Balance:** Encourage work-life balance by implementing flexible work arrangements, promoting time off, and discouraging overwork. Balancing work responsibilities with personal life can help employees better cope with rejection and maintain overall well-being.
7. **Recognize and Celebrate Accomplishments:** Acknowledge employees' achievements and contributions regularly to boost morale and resilience. Recognizing successes can help employees build confidence and resilience, mitigating the impact of rejection.
8. **Offer Professional Development Opportunities:** Provide opportunities for skill development, career advancement, and personal growth. Empowering employees to enhance their skills and pursue their goals can increase resilience and self-confidence in the face of rejection.
9. **Encourage Social Support Networks:** Foster opportunities for employees to connect and support each other, both professionally and socially. Encourage team-building activities, mentorship programs, and peer support networks to provide a sense of belonging and camaraderie.
10. **Lead by Example:** Demonstrate empathy, understanding, and resilience as leaders and managers. Model healthy coping strategies and encourage open dialogue about rejection experiences to create a supportive workplace culture.

Rejection FREE Work Culture

Creating a supportive work culture when dealing with rejection involves fostering an environment where employees feel valued, respected, and supported in managing rejection effectively. Here are steps to create such a culture:

1. **Promote Open Communication:** Encourage open and transparent communication channels where employees feel comfortable expressing their thoughts, feelings, and concerns, including experiences of rejection. Create opportunities for dialogue and feedback to address issues openly and collaboratively.
2. **Cultivate Empathy and Understanding:** Foster empathy and understanding among employees by promoting a culture of respect, compassion, and inclusivity. Encourage individuals to consider the perspectives and feelings of others, especially when providing feedback or addressing rejection-related issues.
3. **Provide Training and Resources:** Offer training programs, workshops, or resources focused on developing skills in emotional intelligence, communication, conflict resolution, and resilience. Equip employees with the tools and techniques needed to navigate rejection effectively and support their colleagues.
4. **Lead by Example:** Model supportive behaviors and interpersonal skills as leaders and managers. Demonstrate empathy, active listening, and constructive feedback in your interactions with others, and encourage these behaviors throughout the organization.
5. **Recognize and Celebrate Contributions:** Acknowledge and celebrate employees' achievements, efforts, and contributions regularly. Recognizing successes and milestones can boost morale, foster a sense of belonging, and reinforce the value of each individual's contributions to the team.
6. **Offer Social Support Networks:** Create opportunities for employees to connect and support each other, both professionally and personally. Encourage team-building activities, mentorship programs, and peer support networks to provide a sense of camaraderie and mutual support.
7. **Promote Work-Life Balance:** Support employees in maintaining a healthy balance between work and personal life by offering flexible work arrangements, promoting time off, and discouraging overwork. Encourage self-care practices and prioritize well-being to help employees manage stress and maintain resilience.
8. **Provide Access to Supportive Resources:** Ensure that employees have access to resources and support services such as counseling, coaching, or employee assistance programs (EAPs) to help them cope with rejection and other challenges. Make sure that employees are aware of these resources and feel comfortable seeking support when needed.
9. **Encourage Continuous Improvement:** Foster a culture of continuous learning and improvement by encouraging feedback, learning from mistakes, and adapting to change. Encourage employees to reflect on their experiences, identify areas for growth, and seek opportunities for development.

By implementing these strategies, organizations can create a supportive work culture that promotes mental health and well-being, empowers employees to navigate rejection effectively, and fosters positive relationships and collaboration within the workplace.

Rejection Free Family Dynamics Solutions

Creating a supportive family environment when dealing with rejection involves fostering a sense of belonging, understanding, and mutual support among family members. Here are steps to create such an environment:

1. **Promote Open Communication:** Encourage open and honest communication within the family, where members feel comfortable expressing their thoughts, feelings, and concerns, including experiences of rejection. Create a safe space for dialogue and validation of emotions.
2. **Demonstrate Empathy and Understanding:** Foster empathy and understanding among family members by actively listening to each other's perspectives and experiences. Encourage empathy by validating emotions, offering support, and showing compassion for one another.
3. **Encourage Emotional Expression:** Validate and encourage the expression of emotions within the family, including sadness, anger, and disappointment. Create an environment where it's okay to talk about feelings and experiences of rejection without fear of judgment or criticism.
4. **Provide Supportive Resources:** Offer support and resources to help family members cope with rejection and its effects. This may include access to counseling, therapy, support groups, or self-help resources to address rejection-related challenges.
5. **Model Healthy Coping Strategies:** Lead by example and model healthy coping strategies for dealing with rejection. Show resilience in the face of setbacks and demonstrate effective problem-solving and emotion regulation skills that family members can emulate.
6. **Promote Mutual Support:** Encourage family members to support each other through difficult times, including experiences of rejection. Foster a sense of solidarity and mutual assistance by offering encouragement, practical help, and emotional support when needed.
7. **Celebrate Achievements and Milestones:** Acknowledge and celebrate family members' accomplishments, successes, and efforts, regardless of the outcome. Celebrating achievements can boost morale, enhance self-esteem, and strengthen family bonds.
8. **Set Realistic Expectations:** Help family members set realistic expectations for themselves and others, recognizing that rejection is a normal part of life and does not define their worth or value as individuals. Encourage resilience and perseverance in the face of setbacks.
9. **Resolve Conflict Constructively:** Teach family members constructive ways to resolve conflicts and disagreements without resorting to rejection or hostility. Encourage active listening, empathy, and compromise to find mutually beneficial solutions.
10. **Create a Sense of Belonging:** Foster a sense of belonging and acceptance within the family by emphasizing unconditional love and support. Encourage family members to embrace their unique identities and strengths, and celebrate diversity within the family unit.

SUMMARY

By implementing these strategies, families can create a supportive environment where members feel understood, valued, and supported in dealing with rejection and other challenges they may face. This supportive family environment can promote resilience, strengthen relationships, and contribute to overall well-being and mental health.

Rejection Work-Life Balance Solutions

Encouraging work-life balance when healing from rejection is essential for promoting overall well-being and resilience. Here are some strategies to encourage work-life balance during this healing process:

1. **Flexible Work Arrangements:** Offer flexible work arrangements such as remote work options, flexible hours, or compressed workweeks to accommodate employees' personal needs and schedules. Flexibility allows individuals to better manage their time and responsibilities, including coping with rejection-related challenges.
2. **Promote Time Off:** Encourage employees to take regular breaks, vacations, and time off to rest, recharge, and focus on self-care. Promote a culture that values and prioritizes time away from work to maintain a healthy work-life balance.
3. **Set Boundaries:** Help employees establish clear boundaries between work and personal life to prevent burnout and maintain well-being. Encourage them to designate specific times and spaces for work-related activities and personal pursuits, and respect these boundaries accordingly.
4. **Lead by Example:** Model healthy work-life balance behaviors as leaders and managers by prioritizing your own well-being and setting boundaries between work and personal life. Demonstrate the importance of self-care and time off by taking breaks, vacations, and time for yourself.
5. **Support Flexible Schedules:** Accommodate employees' personal commitments and responsibilities by allowing for flexible schedules and accommodating requests for time off or schedule adjustments when possible. Recognize that employees have obligations outside of work that may require flexibility.
6. **Encourage Disconnecting:** Encourage employees to disconnect from work during non-work hours, including evenings, weekends, and vacations. Discourage after-hours communication and promote a culture that respects employees' right to rest and recharge outside of work.
7. **Provide Resources and Support:** Offer resources and support to help employees navigate challenges related to work-life balance and rejection. This may include access to counseling, coaching, or employee assistance programs (EAPs) to provide guidance and support during difficult times.
8. **Promote Flexibility in Roles and Responsibilities:** Offer opportunities for job sharing, job rotation, or flexible role assignments to accommodate employees' changing needs and preferences. Allow employees to adjust their responsibilities or workload to better manage their work-life balance.
9. **Regular Check-Ins:** Schedule regular check-ins with employees to discuss their work-life balance, assess their well-being, and address any concerns or challenges they may be facing. Provide opportunities for open dialogue and support to help employees maintain balance and resilience.

SUMMARY

By implementing these strategies, organizations can create a supportive work environment that encourages work-life balance, promotes well-being, and helps employees heal and recover from rejection more effectively.

Rejection Routine Care Solutions

1. **Morning Reflection and Affirmations:** Start the day by reflecting on positive affirmations and intentions. Set aside time each morning to affirm your self-worth, resilience, and capacity for growth. Repeat affirmations such as "I am worthy of love and acceptance," "I am resilient and capable of overcoming challenges," or "I embrace my imperfections and learn from rejection."
2. **Mindful Breathing Exercises:** Practice mindful breathing exercises to promote relaxation and reduce stress. Set aside a few minutes each day to focus on your breath, allowing yourself to become fully present in the moment. Incorporate techniques such as deep breathing, box breathing, or guided imagery to center yourself and cultivate inner peace.
3. **Journaling:** Use journaling as a tool for self-reflection and emotional processing. Set aside time each day to write about your thoughts, feelings, and experiences related to rejection. Explore your emotions without judgment and consider writing down any insights or lessons learned from the experience.
4. **Physical Exercise:** Engage in regular physical exercise to boost mood, reduce stress, and promote overall well-being. Incorporate activities such as walking, jogging, yoga, or dancing into your daily routine. Choose activities that you enjoy and that help you feel energized and empowered.
5. **Creative Expression:** Channel your emotions into creative outlets such as writing, painting, music, or crafting. Expressing yourself creatively can be therapeutic and empowering, allowing you to explore your feelings in a constructive and meaningful way.
6. **Social Connection:** Seek support from friends, family, or support groups who can provide understanding, empathy, and encouragement during difficult times. Make time for social activities and connections that bring you joy and fulfillment, whether it's meeting up with a friend for coffee, joining a community group, or attending a support group meeting.
7. **Self-Care Practices:** Prioritize self-care activities that nourish your body, mind, and spirit. This may include practices such as meditation, mindfulness, taking bubble baths, practicing gratitude, or treating yourself to small indulgences. Make self-care a priority and incorporate it into your daily routine.
8. **Learning and Growth:** Dedicate time to personal growth and learning. Engage in activities that stimulate your mind and expand your perspective, such as reading books, listening to podcasts, attending workshops, or taking up new hobbies. Cultivate a growth mindset and embrace opportunities for learning and development.
9. **Setting Boundaries:** Establish healthy boundaries to protect your emotional well-being and prevent further harm from rejection. Learn to recognize and assert your needs, saying no to situations or relationships that are not in alignment with your values or that may trigger feelings of rejection.

SUMMARY

By incorporating these routines into your daily life, you can support your healing journey from rejection, promote emotional well-being, and cultivate resilience and self-compassion. Adjust and personalize these routines to fit your needs and preferences and remember to be gentle and patient with yourself as you navigate the healing process.

Rejection Free Environment

Creating a rejection-free environment is a challenging but worthwhile endeavor that requires intentional effort and commitment from all individuals involved. Here are some steps to create a rejection-free environment:

1. **Promote Open Communication:** Encourage open and transparent communication among team members, colleagues, or within the community. Create a culture where individuals feel comfortable expressing their thoughts, feelings, and concerns without fear of judgment or reprisal.
2. **Foster a Culture of Respect:** Cultivate a culture of respect, empathy, and inclusivity where all individuals are valued and treated with dignity and kindness. Emphasize the importance of respecting diverse perspectives, backgrounds, and experiences.
3. **Provide Constructive Feedback:** Offer feedback in a constructive and supportive manner that focuses on growth and development rather than criticism or judgment. Encourage feedback to be specific, actionable, and delivered with empathy and respect.
4. **Promote Collaboration and Teamwork:** Encourage collaboration and teamwork among team members or colleagues to foster a sense of belonging and mutual support. Create opportunities for individuals to work together toward common goals and celebrate collective achievements.
5. **Set Realistic Expectations:** Set realistic expectations and goals for individuals and teams, considering their capabilities, resources, and constraints. Avoid setting unattainable standards or unrealistic benchmarks that may lead to feelings of failure or inadequacy.
6. **Celebrate Diversity and Inclusion:** Celebrate diversity and inclusion by embracing the unique strengths, perspectives, and contributions of individuals. Create an environment where differences are celebrated and valued as assets rather than liabilities.
7. **Provide Support and Resources:** Offer support and resources to individuals who may be struggling with rejection or facing challenges. Provide access to counseling, coaching, or other support services to help individuals navigate difficult situations and build resilience.
8. **Lead by Example:** Lead by example as a role model of positive behavior and attitudes. Demonstrate empathy, humility, and resilience in your interactions with others, and foster a culture of kindness, understanding, and acceptance.
9. **Encourage Self-Care:** Promote self-care practices that help individuals manage stress, maintain balance, and prioritize their well-being. Encourage individuals to take breaks, engage in hobbies, and seek support when needed to prevent burnout and promote overall health and resilience.
10. **Address Issues Promptly:** Address issues of discrimination, harassment, or unfair treatment promptly and effectively. Take concerns seriously, investigate complaints thoroughly, and take appropriate action to address and prevent recurrence of such behavior.

Creating a rejection-free environment requires ongoing effort, collaboration, and commitment from all individuals involved. By fostering open communication, respect, collaboration, and support, you can create an environment where individuals feel valued, empowered, and respected, and where rejection is minimized or addressed constructively.

Dealing with Rejection
Do and Don't

Do:

1. **Do Acknowledge Your Feelings:** Acknowledge and validate your emotions in response to rejection. It's natural to feel hurt, disappointed, or upset, and it's important to give yourself permission to experience and express these feelings.
2. **Do Practice Self-Compassion:** Be kind and compassionate toward yourself during times of rejection. Treat yourself with the same empathy and understanding that you would offer to a friend in a similar situation.
3. **Do Seek Support:** Reach out to friends, family members, or trusted colleagues for support and encouragement. Sharing your feelings with others can provide validation, perspective, and comfort during difficult times.
4. **Do Learn from Rejection:** Use rejection as an opportunity for growth and learning. Reflect on the feedback or experiences that led to the rejection and identify areas for improvement or alternative strategies for future endeavors.
5. **Do Maintain Perspective:** Maintain a balanced perspective on rejection by recognizing that it's often a temporary setback rather than a reflection of your worth or abilities. Focus on your strengths, accomplishments, and potential for success in the future.

Don't:

1. **Don't Take it Personally:** Avoid taking rejection personally or internalizing it as a reflection of your identity or value as a person. Recognize that rejection is often subjective and influenced by various factors beyond your control.
2. **Don't Ruminate or Obsess:** Avoid getting caught up in rumination or obsessive thoughts about rejection. Dwelling on the past or replaying the rejection scenario in your mind repeatedly can increase feelings of distress and hinder your ability to move forward.
3. **Don't Compare Yourself to Others:** Resist the urge to compare yourself to others who may have experienced success or avoided rejection. Remember that everyone faces rejection at some point in their lives, and it's not a reflection of your worth or potential.
4. **Don't Give Up:** Refrain from giving up on your goals or aspirations in the face of rejection. Use rejection as motivation to persevere, adapt, and continue pursuing your dreams with resilience and determination.
5. **Don't Seek Validation from Rejection:** Avoid seeking validation or self-worth solely from external sources, such as approval or acceptance from others. Instead, focus on cultivating self-confidence and self-validation from within, independent of **external validation**.

Rejection Critical Conversation Solutions

Having the right conversation after experiencing rejection is crucial for maintaining mutual respect, clarity, and potentially salvaging the relationship or situation. Here are some steps to guide you:

1. **Prepare Emotionally:** Take some time to process your emotions and gain clarity about your feelings and intentions before initiating the conversation. It's important to approach the conversation from a place of calmness and clarity rather than impulsiveness or reactivity.
2. **Choose the Right Time and Place:** Select a time and place where both parties can engage in a private, uninterrupted conversation. Ensure that you have enough time to discuss the matter fully without feeling rushed or distracted.
3. **Start with Empathy and Understanding:** Begin the conversation by expressing empathy and understanding towards the other person's perspective. Acknowledge that rejection can be difficult for both parties and validate any emotions they may be experiencing.
4. **Be Honest and Transparent:** Be honest and transparent about your own feelings, thoughts, and intentions regarding rejection. Clearly articulate your perspective, concerns, and any questions you may have. Avoid blaming or accusing the other person and focus on expressing your own experiences and needs.
5. **Listen Actively:** Practice active listening by giving the other person your full attention and genuinely seeking to understand their perspective. Allow them to express their thoughts and feelings without interruption and validate their experiences and concerns.
6. **Seek Clarification and Understanding:** Ask clarifying questions to gain a deeper understanding of the reasons behind the rejection and the other person's motivations or intentions. Seek to clarify any misunderstandings and ensure that both parties are on the same page.
7. **Explore Possible Solutions or Next Steps:** Brainstorm together to explore possible solutions or next steps that may address the concerns or issues raised during the conversation. Be open to compromise, negotiation, or finding common ground that respects the needs and boundaries of both parties.
8. **Express Gratitude and Respect:** Regardless of the outcome of the conversation, express gratitude and respect towards the other person for their willingness to engage in an open and honest dialogue. Acknowledge any insights or lessons learned from the conversation and express a commitment to moving forward positively.
9. **Follow-Up as Needed:** Depending on the outcome of the conversation, follow up as needed to address any unresolved issues, provide updates, or further clarify expectations. Maintain open lines of communication and be willing to revisit the conversation as needed in the future.

By approaching the conversation with empathy, honesty, and a willingness to listen and understand, you can have a productive and respectful dialogue after experiencing rejection. This can help foster mutual understanding, clarity, and potentially lead to positive outcomes or resolution.

Breaking Rejection Cycle

To avoid the vicious cycle of rejection, it's important to implement proactive strategies and mindset shifts that promote resilience, self-awareness, and positive self-esteem. Here are some tips to break free from the cycle of rejection:

1. **Challenge Negative Self-Talk:** Recognize and challenge negative self-talk or limiting beliefs that perpetuate feelings of inadequacy or unworthiness. Replace negative thoughts with positive affirmations and realistic self-appraisals.
2. **Cultivate Self-Compassion:** Practice self-compassion by treating yourself with kindness, understanding, and acceptance, especially in moments of disappointment or failure. Offer yourself the same empathy and support that you would offer to a friend in a similar situation.
3. **Focus on Personal Growth:** Shift your focus from seeking external validation to prioritizing personal growth and self-improvement. Set meaningful goals, pursue your passions, and focus on continuous learning and development.
4. **Seek Feedback and Learn from Rejection:** Instead of viewing rejection as a reflection of your worth, see it as an opportunity for growth and learning. Seek feedback from rejection experiences and use them as valuable insights to improve and refine your skills and approach.
5. **Build Resilience:** Cultivate resilience by developing coping strategies and resilience-building techniques, such as mindfulness, gratitude, and problem-solving skills. Build a support network of friends, family, or mentors who can provide encouragement and perspective during challenging times.
6. **Set Realistic Expectations:** Avoid setting unrealistic expectations for yourself or others, as this can set you up for disappointment and perpetuate the cycle of rejection. Set achievable goals and celebrate progress, no matter how small.
7. **Practice Boundary Setting:** Establish healthy boundaries in your relationships and interactions to protect your emotional well-being and prevent further rejection. Learn to assert your needs and prioritize your own self-care and happiness.
8. **Focus on What You Can Control:** Focus on aspects of your life that you can control, such as your attitude, actions, and responses to situations. Let go of things beyond your control and channel your energy into areas where you can make a positive difference.
9. **Embrace Failure as a Learning Opportunity:** Shift your mindset towards failure as a natural part of the learning process rather than a reflection of your abilities. Embrace failure as an opportunity to gain valuable insights, build resilience, and ultimately achieve success.
10. **Seek Professional Help if Needed:** If you find yourself trapped in a cycle of rejection that is impacting your mental health and well-being, don't hesitate to seek professional help from a therapist or counselor. They can provide guidance, support, and strategies to help you break free from the cycle and cultivate a healthier mindset.

By implementing these strategies and mindset shifts, you can break free from the vicious cycle of rejection and cultivate a more resilient, self-aware, and empowered approach to life's challenges.

Rejection Care Solutions

1. **Self-Awareness:** Develop self-awareness to recognize personal triggers and vulnerabilities related to rejection. Understanding one's own reactions and patterns can help in implementing preventive measures.
2. **Healthy Boundaries:** Establish and maintain healthy boundaries in relationships and interactions. Clear boundaries can help protect against potential rejection and maintain emotional well-being.
3. **Effective Communication:** Practice open, honest, and assertive communication to express needs, set expectations, and address concerns. Clear communication can help prevent misunderstandings and minimize the risk of rejection.
4. **Conflict Resolution Skills:** Develop skills in conflict resolution and problem-solving to address issues in relationships and interactions constructively. Effective conflict resolution can prevent escalation and reduce the likelihood of rejection.
5. **Social Support Networks:** Cultivate supportive relationships with friends, family, and peers who can provide encouragement, empathy, and validation. Strong social support networks can buffer against the negative effects of rejection.
6. **Self-Care Practices:** Prioritize self-care activities that promote physical, emotional, and mental well-being, such as exercise, relaxation techniques, hobbies, and leisure activities. Engaging in self-care can enhance resilience and coping abilities.
7. **Positive Self-Talk:** Practice positive self-talk and self-affirmations to challenge negative beliefs and build self-confidence. Cultivating a positive self-image can help protect against the impact of rejection on self-esteem.
8. **Mindfulness and Acceptance:** Develop mindfulness skills to cultivate present-moment awareness and acceptance of thoughts, emotions, and experiences. Mindfulness can help individuals cope with rejection by fostering acceptance and resilience.
9. **Flexible Thinking:** Cultivate a mindset of flexibility and adaptability in response to rejection. Embrace setbacks as opportunities for growth and learning, rather than viewing them as personal failures.
10. **Seeking Feedback:** Proactively seek feedback from others to gain insights into areas for improvement and growth. Constructive feedback can provide valuable information for enhancing social skills and interpersonal relationships.
11. **Setting Realistic Expectations:** Set realistic expectations for oneself and others in relationships and interactions. Recognize that not every interaction will result in acceptance or approval, and that rejection is a normal part of life.
12. **Engaging in Activities:** Participate in activities and pursuits that bring joy, fulfillment, and a sense of accomplishment. Engaging in meaningful activities can provide a sense of purpose and connection, reducing the impact of rejection.

By incorporating these preventive care strategies into daily life, individuals can build resilience, strengthen social connections, and minimize the impact of rejection on their overall well-being.

Rejection Breathing Techniques

In our journey through life, we inevitably encounter moments of rejection – whether it's in our personal relationships, professional endeavors, or even within ourselves. Rejection can evoke a range of emotions, from sadness and disappointment to anxiety and self-doubt. These feelings can be overwhelming and challenging to navigate, often leaving us feeling stressed, tense, and emotionally drained. However, amidst the turmoil of rejection, there exists a powerful tool that can help us find solace, regain composure, and foster resilience: breathing techniques.

Breathing techniques have been utilized for centuries as a means of promoting relaxation, reducing stress, and enhancing overall well-being. By harnessing the power of the breath, we can tap into the body's natural ability to calm the mind, soothe the spirit, and restore balance in times of distress. When it comes to dealing with rejection, the importance of utilizing breathing techniques cannot be overstated. These techniques offer a simple yet effective way to ground ourselves, center our thoughts, and navigate the turbulent waters of rejection with greater ease and clarity.

In this guide, we will explore the significance of using rejection breathing techniques as part of a comprehensive approach to managing rejection. We will delve into the physiological and psychological effects of breathing on the body and mind, highlighting how intentional breathing can help regulate emotions, alleviate stress, and promote emotional resilience in the face of rejection. Through practical exercises, tips, and strategies, we will learn how to harness the healing power to cultivate a sense of calmness, confidence, and inner strength when confronted with rejection. Whether you're seeking relief from rejection-related stress, looking to enhance your coping skills, or simply striving to cultivate a greater sense of well-being in your life, mastering rejection breathing techniques can be a valuable tool on your journey toward healing and growth.

Rejection Breathing Exercises Benefits

The benefits of using the breathing exercises for dealing with rejection includes:

1. **Regulates Emotions:** Breathing exercises help regulate emotions by activating the body's relaxation response. When faced with rejection, emotions such as sadness, anger, or anxiety can run high. Deep breathing helps calm the nervous system, reducing the intensity of these emotions and promoting a sense of calmness and clarity.
2. **Reduces Stress:** Rejection can be a significant source of stress, triggering the body's "fight or flight" response. Chronic stress can have detrimental effects on physical and mental health. Breathing exercises counteract the stress response by promoting relaxation and reducing levels of stress hormones such as cortisol, helping to alleviate the physiological effects of rejection.
3. **Promotes Mindfulness:** Breathing exercises cultivate mindfulness, the practice of being fully present in the moment without judgment. Mindfulness allows individuals to observe their thoughts and feelings without becoming overwhelmed by them. By focusing on the breath, individuals can anchor themselves in the present moment, reducing rumination and fostering a greater sense of acceptance and self-awareness.
4. **Enhances Coping Skills:** Learning to use breathing exercises as a coping mechanism builds resilience and adaptive coping skills. Instead of reacting impulsively or succumbing to negative emotions, individuals can use breathing techniques to respond to rejection in a calm and composed manner. This empowers individuals to approach challenges with greater clarity, creativity, and resourcefulness.
5. **Improves Physical Health:** In addition to its mental health benefits, breathing exercises have numerous physical health benefits. Deep breathing increases oxygen flow to the brain and body, promoting relaxation, reducing muscle tension, and improving overall well-being. Regular practice of breathing exercises can contribute to better cardiovascular health, immune function, and overall vitality.
6. **Provides a Sense of Control:** Rejection can leave individuals feeling powerless and vulnerable. Breathing exercises offer a sense of control in the midst of adversity. By focusing on the breath, individuals reclaim agency over their internal state, empowering them to manage their emotions and navigate rejection more effectively.
7. **Facilitates Healing and Recovery:** Breathing exercises play a role in the healing and recovery process following rejection. They provide a gentle and accessible means of self-care and self-soothing, promoting emotional healing and facilitating the integration of rejection experiences into one's personal narrative. By fostering self-compassion and self-acceptance, breathing exercises support individuals in moving forward with resilience and grace.

Rejection Technique

This breathing technique can be a valuable tool for managing rejection-related stress and promoting relaxation and resilience. As part of a comprehensive rejection treatment plan, it can help individuals cultivate a sense of calmness and inner peace, empowering them to navigate rejection more effectively.

1. **Find a Comfortable Position:** Sit or lie down in a comfortable position, with your back straight and your hands resting comfortably in your lap or on your thighs.
2. **Close Your Eyes:** Close your eyes gently to minimize distractions and focus your attention inward.
3. **Deep Belly Breaths:** Begin by taking a few deep breaths, focusing on filling your belly with air rather than your chest. Inhale deeply through your nose, allowing your abdomen to expand fully. Hold the breath for a moment at the top of the inhalation.
4. **Slow Exhalation:** Exhale slowly and completely through your mouth, allowing your abdomen to deflate as you release the breath. Focus on releasing any tension or stress with each exhalation.
5. **Counting Breath Cycles:** As you continue to breathe deeply and rhythmically, you can incorporate a counting technique to help focus your mind and regulate your breathing. Counting to four during each inhalation and exhalation can help establish a steady rhythm.
6. **Visualize Relaxation:** With each breath cycle, visualize a sense of relaxation spreading throughout your body. Imagine tension melting away from your muscles, leaving you feeling calm, grounded, and at ease.
7. **Repeat:** Continue this deep breathing technique for several minutes, allowing yourself to fully relax and unwind. If your mind wanders, gently redirect your focus back to your breath and the present moment.
8. **Reflect:** After completing the breathing exercise, take a moment to reflect on how you feel. Notice any changes in your body, emotions, or mental state. Acknowledge any feelings of calmness or relaxation that may have emerged.
9. **Practice Regularly:** Incorporate this breathing technique into your daily routine, especially during times of stress or when facing situations that may trigger feelings of rejection. With regular practice, you can strengthen your ability to manage rejection effectively and promote your overall well-being.

SUMMARY

Overall, the importance of using breathing exercises for dealing with rejection lies in their ability to promote emotional regulation, reduce stress, enhance coping skills, and foster overall well-being. Incorporating breathing exercises into a comprehensive rejection treatment plan can be a valuable tool for individuals seeking to navigate rejection with greater ease, resilience, and self-compassion.

Reject Rejection

Reject rejection before it beats you" encapsulates the proactive mindset needed to overcome rejection and emerge stronger from adversity. By refusing to succumb to feelings of defeat or inadequacy, individuals can reclaim their power and resilience. The key is to adopt a proactive approach, acknowledging rejection as a natural part of life while refusing to let it define one's worth or potential. Instead, individuals can use rejection as motivation for growth, learning, and self-improvement. By cultivating self-confidence, resilience, and a positive mindset, individuals can reject rejection before it has the chance to undermine their confidence and hinder their progress. Ultimately, this mindset empowers individuals to embrace challenges, pursue their goals with determination, and thrive in the face of adversity.

Stop Rejection

Stopping rejection before it stops you emphasizes the proactive approach needed to address rejection and prevent it from undermining one's confidence and progress. It involves recognizing rejection as a temporary setback rather than a reflection of one's worth or potential. By cultivating resilience, self-awareness, and a positive mindset, individuals can preemptively reject rejection by refusing to let it define their identity or dictate their future. This proactive stance enables individuals to embrace challenges, learn from setbacks, and pursue their goals with confidence and determination. Ultimately, by taking control of their own narrative and refusing to be defined by rejection, individuals can overcome obstacles and thrive in the face of adversity.

Rejection Normalization Cards

Normalization cards for rejection are designed to help individuals recognize that rejection is a common and natural experience that everyone encounters at some point in their lives. Here's how to develop normalization cards:

1. **Positive Affirmations:** Create cards with positive affirmations that normalize the experience of rejection. Examples include:
   - "Rejection is a natural part of life and does not define my worth."
   - "Everyone experiences rejection at some point, and it's okay to feel disappointed."
   - "Rejection is an opportunity for growth and self-discovery."
2. **Famous Examples:** Include cards with examples of well-known individuals who have experienced rejection before achieving success. This can help individuals realize that rejection is not a reflection of their abilities or potential. Examples may include:
   - J.K. Rowling, whose Harry Potter manuscript was rejected by multiple publishers before becoming a bestseller.
   - Walt Disney, who was fired from a newspaper job for lacking creativity before founding Disney Studios.

3. **Statistics:** Provide cards with statistics or data on the prevalence of rejection in various aspects of life. This can help individuals understand that they are not alone in their experiences. Examples include:
    - "Studies show that job applicants receive an average of 24 rejections before landing a job offer."
    - "Over 50% of romantic relationships end in rejection or breakup."
4. **Personal Stories:** Share cards with personal anecdotes or stories from individuals who have overcome rejection. These stories can offer encouragement and inspiration to those struggling with rejection. Encourage individuals to share their own stories as well, fostering a sense of empathy and connection.
5. **Coping Strategies:** Include cards with practical coping strategies for dealing with rejection. This may include:
    - "Practice self-care activities such as exercise, meditation, or spending time with loved ones."
    - "Seek support from friends, family, or a therapist to talk about your feelings and gain perspective."
    - "Focus on your strengths and accomplishments to boost your self-confidence and resilience."
6. **Encouragement:** Offer cards with words of encouragement and reassurance to lift spirits and instill hope. Examples include:
    - "You are resilient and capable of overcoming rejection."
    - "Every rejection brings you one step closer to success."
    - "Believe in yourself and your ability to overcome obstacles."

SUMMARY

By developing normalization cards for rejection, individuals can gain a more balanced perspective on rejection and learn to navigate it with resilience, self-compassion, and determination.

Church Rejection Rules

1. **Acknowledge Your Feelings:** Allow yourself to feel and process the emotions that come with rejection, such as sadness, disappointment, or frustration. Avoid suppressing or denying your feelings, as this can prolong the healing process.
2. **Practice Self-Compassion:** Be kind and gentle with yourself during times of rejection. Treat yourself with the same empathy and understanding that you would offer to a friend in a similar situation. Avoid self-blame or harsh self-criticism.
3. **Avoid Rumination:** While it's natural to reflect on the rejection and its impact, avoid excessive rumination or dwelling on negative thoughts. Set boundaries for how much time you allow yourself to dwell on the rejection, and actively redirect your focus to more positive or productive activities.
4. **Seek Perspective:** Gain perspective on the rejection by considering the bigger picture and recognizing that it is not a reflection of your entire worth or identity. Seek feedback or advice from trusted friends, family members, or mentors to gain additional perspective on the situation.
5. **Learn from Experience:** Use rejection as an opportunity for growth and self-improvement. Reflect on what you can learn from the experience and how you can use it to inform your future actions or decisions. Look for silver linings or lessons learned that can help you move forward positively.
6. **Maintain Boundaries:** Set boundaries in your relationships and interactions to protect your emotional well-being and prevent further rejection. Be assertive in expressing your needs and boundaries and avoid placing unrealistic expectations on yourself or others.
7. **Focus on What You Can Control:** Shift your focus to aspects of the situation that you can control, such as your attitude, actions, and responses. Let go of things beyond your control, such as other people's opinions or decisions, and channel your energy into areas where you can make a positive difference.
8. **Practice Resilience:** Cultivate resilience by developing coping strategies and resilience-building techniques, such as mindfulness, gratitude, and positive self-talk. Build a support network of friends, family, or mentors who can provide encouragement and perspective during difficult times.
9. **Stay Positive:** Maintain a positive outlook and believe in your ability to overcome challenges and bounce back from rejection. Focus on your strengths and accomplishments and remind yourself of past instances where you have overcome obstacles.
10. **Keep Moving Forward:** Finally, don't let rejection hold you back from pursuing your goals and aspirations. Stay focused on your dreams and aspirations and take proactive steps towards achieving them. Remember that rejection is a temporary setback, and with resilience and determination, you can overcome it and thrive in the long run.

Church Rejection Diary Worksheet

To develop a rejection diary worksheet, consider the following elements:

1. **Date and Time:** Provide space for individuals to record the date and time of the rejection experience. This helps track patterns and identify trends over time.
2. **Description of Rejection:** Encourage individuals to describe the rejection experience in detail. This may include the context of the rejection (e.g., job application, romantic relationship), the specific interaction or event, and any feedback received.
3. **Emotional Response:** Have individuals reflect on their emotional response to the rejection. Ask them to identify and describe the emotions they felt during and after the experience (e.g., sadness, anger, disappointment).
4. **Thoughts and Beliefs:** Prompt individuals to explore their thoughts and beliefs about themselves and the rejection. Encourage them to identify any negative or self-critical thoughts that emerged as a result of the rejection.
5. **Coping Strategies:** Have individuals list the coping strategies they used to deal with the rejection. This may include activities they engaged in to manage their emotions (e.g., talking to a friend, journaling) or strategies for reframing their thoughts (e.g., practicing self-compassion, challenging negative beliefs).
6. **Outcome:** Encourage individuals to reflect on the outcome of the rejection experience. Did they learn anything from the experience? Did they take any positive steps forward despite the rejection?
7. **Lessons Learned:** Prompt individuals to identify any lessons or insights they gained from the rejection experience. This could include recognizing patterns in their responses to rejection, discovering new coping strategies, or gaining perspective on their strengths and areas for growth.
8. **Future Action:** Have individuals consider how they can use the insights gained from the rejection experience to inform their future actions and decisions. Encourage them to set goals for how they want to approach similar situations in the future.
9. **Reflection:** Provide space for individuals to reflect on their overall experience with the rejection diary worksheet. This could include noting any changes in their mindset or behavior over time, as well as expressing gratitude for any positive outcomes or growth that resulted from the rejection.

By completing the rejection diary worksheet, individuals can gain greater self-awareness, process their emotions more effectively, and develop proactive strategies for coping with rejection in the future.

Building Tolerance for Church Rejection

Building tolerance for rejection is a crucial skill that empowers individuals to navigate life's challenges with resilience and confidence. This process involves developing the capacity to accept rejection as a natural part of life and to respond to setbacks with grace and resilience. By reframing rejection as an opportunity for growth and learning, individuals can build resilience and self-confidence, enabling them to persevere in the face of adversity. Building tolerance for rejection requires self-awareness, emotional regulation, and a willingness to embrace discomfort. Through proactive strategies such as setting realistic expectations, practicing self-compassion, and seeking support from others, individuals can cultivate greater resilience and thrive in the face of rejection. Ultimately, building tolerance for rejection is not about avoiding rejection altogether, but rather about developing the inner strength and resilience to navigate rejection with confidence and grace.

Church Rejection Summary

In conclusion, "**Reject Rejection**" serves as a guiding light for individuals navigating the tumultuous waters of rejection. By providing practical strategies, heartfelt insights, and a compassionate approach, this manual offers a roadmap to not only endure rejection but to transcend it. As we journey through life's inevitable ups and downs, may we remember that rejection does not define us, but rather shapes us into resilient, empathetic beings capable of growth and transformation. With the wisdom gained from "Reject Rejection," may we embrace rejection as a catalyst for self-discovery and empowerment, ultimately leading us to a place of greater fulfillment and authenticity.

Rejection Questionnaire

The Rejection Triggers Questionnaire

Instructions for Completing the Rejection Triggers Questionnaire: As you embark on completing the Rejection Triggers Questionnaire, take a moment to center yourself and reflect on your past experiences with rejection. Each question is designed to delve into different aspects of rejection triggers, emotions, coping mechanisms, and insights gained from your experiences. Be open and honest in your responses, as this will help you gain deeper insights into your own triggers and coping strategies. Take your time to consider each question thoughtfully, and feel free to provide examples or anecdotes to illustrate your responses if it helps clarify your thoughts. Remember that exploring feelings of rejection can sometimes bring up challenging emotions, so be kind and compassionate toward yourself throughout the process. Once you've completed the questionnaire, take a moment to review your responses and consider what insights you've gained. If you find that certain questions evoke strong emotions or raise concerns, don't hesitate to reach out to a trusted friend, family member, or mental health professional for support and guidance. Your willingness to engage in this process of self-reflection is a powerful step toward understanding and navigating rejection more effectively in your life.

Rejection Triggers Questionnaire

1.	Have you experienced rejection in the past? If yes, please briefly describe the situation(s).
2.	In your opinion, what does rejection mean to you?
3.	Think back to a recent experience of rejection.
4.	What emotions did you feel during that time?
5.	What types of situations or interactions tend to trigger feelings of rejection for you?
6.	How do you typically react when you perceive rejection in a situation?
7.	Have you noticed any patterns or themes in the types of rejections you experience?
8.	Reflect on your past experiences of rejection.
9.	Are there any common factors or underlying reasons that seem to contribute to those rejections?
10.	How do you cope with feelings of rejection?
11.	Do you have any strategies or techniques that help you navigate those emotions?
12.	Have you ever confronted someone about their behavior or decisions that made you feel rejected?
13.	If so, how did that conversation go?
14.	Are there any specific triggers or situations that you try to avoid to prevent feelings of rejection?
15.	How do your past experiences of rejection influence your behavior or interactions in present situations?
16.	Reflect on a time when you overcame feelings of rejection.
17.	What strategies or resources did you find helpful in overcoming those emotions?
18.	Do you have a support system or network of people you can turn to for help or guidance when dealing with rejection?
19.	What advice would you give to someone who is struggling with feelings of rejection? Is there anything else you would like to share about your experiences with rejection and how it affects you?

SUMMARY

Upon completing the rejection questionnaire, we have embarked on a journey of self-reflection and introspection, delving into the intricate dynamics of rejection triggers. Through honest and thoughtful responses, we have gained insights into our past experiences with rejection, our emotional responses, and our coping mechanisms. By identifying common triggers and patterns, we have deepened our understanding of how rejection impacts us and how we navigate these challenging emotions. Armed with this newfound self-awareness, we are better equipped to recognize and address rejection triggers in our lives, fostering resilience and fostering healthier relationships. As we move forward, let us continue to cultivate empathy, compassion, and self-care, knowing that our journey toward healing and growth is ongoing.

Resources

These websites offer a range of resources, articles, and support for individuals seeking guidance and strategies for navigating rejection and building resilience.

- Rejection Therapy (https://www.rejectiontherapy.com/): Offers resources, challenges, and strategies for overcoming the fear of rejection and building resilience.
- Psychology Today - Coping with Rejection (https://www.psychologytoday.com/us/basics/rejection): Provides articles, tips, and expert advice on coping with rejection and building emotional resilience.
- Greater Good Magazine - Overcoming Rejection (https://greatergood.berkeley.edu/topic/rejection): Offers research-based articles and resources on understanding and overcoming rejection.
- Mindful - Navigating Rejection (https://www.mindful.org/search/rejection/): Features articles, guided meditations, and practices for navigating rejection with mindfulness and compassion.
- TED Talks - Dealing with Rejection (https://www.ted.com/topics/rejection): Curates TED Talks on overcoming rejection, building resilience, and finding strength in the face of adversity.
- ReachOut.com - Dealing with Rejection (https://au.reachout.com/articles/dealing-with-rejection): Provides articles, forums, and tools for young people dealing with rejection and relationship challenges.
- HelpGuide - Coping with Rejection (https://www.helpguide.org/articles/relationships-communication/coping-with-rejection.htm): Offers tips, strategies, and resources for coping with rejection and maintaining emotional well-being.
- The Gottman Institute - Handling Rejection (https://www.gottman.com/blog/tag/rejection/): Features articles and resources on navigating rejection in relationships and building healthy connections.
- Verywell Mind - Understanding Rejection (https://www.verywellmind.com/search?q=rejection): Provides articles, quizzes, and expert insights on understanding and coping with rejection in various life situations.

About the Author

DR. RICHELLE MCMILLAN

Dr. **Richelle R. McMillan** is a native of Durham, North Carolina. Dr. McMillan has been instrumental in overseeing various departments within the community and different ministries. She has assisted with implementing viable children's tutoring programs within several organizations. She has had the opportunity to train numerous organizational departments on specific topics such as servant leadership styles. Dr. McMillan is the founder and President of Richelle McMillan Enterprise, LLC. This new initiative is a monumental ministry called the Spiritual Sons & Daughters Movement. This platform entitled *Pathway 2 Me* empower women all over the world through mailing over 200 monthly hand-written personalized inspirational postcards, hosting weekly conference calls, collaborating with agencies from delivering food boxes to making handmade chemo caps, gloves, and scarves for seniors. She has made a commitment to equipping women around the country to reach their zenith and find their purpose in life. Dr. McMillan is known for her clever mentoring and leadership style instills in people that their life is a vast opportunity of unlimited possibilities! She is very involved in community activities and has a desire to move people towards discipleship and spiritual leadership through worship, ministry, and edification. The breath of her talents extends to being a published author of seven books. She is the published author of books titled *"The Gifts of Life Nobody Wants", All Eyes On Me to Achieve My Destiny, Behind Closed Doors: Married to the Church, My Wife is My Mistress, The Jesus Chair, Married to the Church, My Wife is My Mistress Sequel, SO, You Want to Date Me and Why am I still Sin-Gle?* She resides on the Florida coast of Orange Park, Fl with her two beautiful daughters.

Made in the USA
Columbia, SC
12 February 2025